RAND ARROYO CENTER

T0302757

Prospective Outcome Assessment for Alternative Recruit Selection Policies

Bruce R. Orvis, Christopher E. Maerzluft, Sung-Bou Kim,
Michael G. Shanley, Heather Krull

Prepared for the United States Army
Approved for public release; distribution unlimited

For more information on this publication, visit www.rand.org/t/RR2267

Library of Congress Control Number: 2018947699
ISBN: 978-0-8330-9988-4

Published by the RAND Corporation, Santa Monica, Calif.

Preface

This report documents research and analysis conducted as part of a project entitled "Optimizing Recruits Screening, Qualification Standards, and Preparation for Training," sponsored by the Assistant Secretary of the Army for Manpower and Reserve Affairs, and the Deputy Chief of Staff, G-1, U.S. Army. The purpose of the project was to provide the Army with a means of identifying the prospective effects of combinations of new recruits' cognitive, noncognitive, physical, demographic, and behavioral attributes on serving successfully and completing their first term, and on related costs, thus enabling the Army to identify potential changes to selection of youth based on these attributes in order to expand supply smartly or to decrease the rates of targeted adverse outcomes.

The Project Unique Identification Code (PUIC) for the project that produced this document is RAN167280.

This research was conducted within RAND Arroyo Center's Personnel, Training, and Health Program. RAND Arroyo Center, part of the RAND Corporation, is a federally funded research and development center (FFRDC) sponsored by the United States Army.

RAND operates under a "Federal-Wide Assurance" (FWA00003425) and complies with the *Code of Federal Regulations for the Protection of Human Subjects Under United States Law* (45 CFR 46), also known as "the Common Rule," as well as with the implementation guidance set forth in Department of Defense Instruction 3216.02. As applicable, this compliance includes reviews and approvals by RAND's Institutional Review Board (the Human Subjects Protection Committee) and by the U.S. Army. The views of sources utilized in this report are solely their own and do not represent the official policy or position of the U.S. Department of Defense or the U.S. government.

Contents

Figures and Tables

Figures

Tables

Summary

Successful completion of the first term of enlistment (or the contract term for recruits with prior service) is very important for both readiness and minimizing cost. Selecting recruits who do not complete their first term is unnecessarily expensive and inefficient, because the Army is expending recruiting and Initial Entry Training (IET) resources on soldiers whose experience is lost and who must be replaced with new recruits. Despite implementation of higher recruiting standards, changes to enlistment policy, and a Future Soldier Training Program, the Army continues to experience 30–35 percent attrition over the first term of active federal service. A significant amount of research has examined this problem, and enlistment policy often is based on this research. However, this research has often examined a limited number of predictors in isolation, whereas research and tools that consider multiple factors and how various factors work in combination are necessary to develop more-successful recruit selection policies.

This report describes a recruit selection tool that estimates prospective outcomes and costs for different combinations of recruits' cognitive, noncognitive, demographic, physical, and behavioral attributes. The tool enables the Army to assess the prospective, joint effects of multiple, simultaneous changes in the selection of prospects on losses during the Delayed Entry Program (DEP), IET, or later in first term; on the incidence of adverse personnel actions, such as a bar to reenlistment, demotion, or suspension of favorable person status; and on specific reasons for early separation from the Army, such as those relating to performance, conduct, or medical factors. The tool

- can identify combinations of changes in selection rates across prospects' attributes that are likely to (1) lower or limit increases in attrition during the DEP, IET, and first term and (2) help the Army reduce or limit other adverse outcomes
- considers recruiting, training costs, and replacement costs and, as appropriate, Regular Military Compensation (RMC) differences
- can provide insights into large differences in potential costs and into the relationship between changes in the rates of adverse outcomes and changes in costs, which do not always move in the same direction
- can consider environments requiring increased supply, as well as environments in which fewer recruits are needed and selection rates can be reduced to lower attrition or other problem behaviors.

The research proceeded in several steps. First, we reviewed the literature examining (1) the relationship between soldiers' characteristics at enlistment (such as demographic factors, education level and aptitude, physical- and health-related factors, noncognitive factors, medical and conduct waivers, prior service, and test scores) and attrition from the DEP, IET, and their first term, (2) relationships to intermediate adverse personnel action outcomes (such as a bar to reenlistment), which can be related to subsequent separation from the Army, and (3) specific reasons for early separation. We then integrated these findings.

Using available, recent data, we then quantified the association of each enlistment characteristic identified in the literature separately with DEP, training, and overall first-term attrition. These characteristics included educational attainment, Armed Forces Qualification Test score, type of waiver, noncognitive/compensatory selection measures (e.g., Tier Two Attrition Screen, Assessment of Recruit Motivation and Strength), body mass index/physical condition, time in DEP, prior service, and demographics. In addition to the associations of the individual enlistment characteristics with loss rates and the timing of the losses, the study team examined the coded reasons for losses. We also analyzed the relationships between enlistment characteristics and adverse intermediate personnel outcomes.

We then modeled the joint associations of the enlistment characteristics found to be most important with the rates, timing, and reasons for losses and with adverse personnel outcomes when controlling for recruits' levels on the other primary characteristics. Using the factors found to be the primary drivers of the outcomes in the regression results, all else equal, we built a tool to simulate the effects of alternative combinations of recruit characteristics on attrition during the DEP, IET, and in the first term (or the contract term for recruits with prior service), considering both the timing (within specific training courses, during training overall, during post-training [in units], and overall attrition during the term) and the reason for attrition. The tool also simulates the effects of alternative combinations of recruit characteristics on adverse intermediate outcomes. It quantifies recruiting, training, and replacement costs associated with these alternative combinations. Possible differences in compensation costs associated with these changes also are considered when the number of recruits with prior military service is changed.

The tool enables the user to strategically examine trade-offs among changes in the characteristics of the recruit cohort, recruit outcomes, and related costs to the Army. It can identify combinations of recruit characteristics likely to help to lower or limit increases in attrition and other adverse outcomes during the DEP, IET, and first term, and do so in a manner such that the eligible recruit pool is expanded or not overly constricted. In some instances, costs can be lowered, even though loss rates increase, due to trade-offs among recruiting, training, and replacement costs. Conversely, costs can increase even when attrition rates fall. As discussed in the report, in setting appropriate recruit eligibility policies, the trade-offs between outcomes and costs and, particularly on the cost side, between replacement costs and recruiting costs, depend not only on the characteristics of the accession cohort but on the number of accessions needed and the difficulty of the recruiting environment.

Acknowledgments

Many people contributed their talents and insight into the development of the recruit selection tool. In particular, we wish to thank COL Joanne Moore (G-1), Shawn McCurry and John Jessup (Army Marketing and Research Group), and Rick Ayer and Todd Sherman (U.S. Army Recruiting Command) for their support and insights. At RAND, Laurie McDonald, Rodger Madison, and David Knapp provided us critical data that allowed us to estimate our models and outcomes. We also are grateful to our reviewers, Matthew Goldberg (Institute for Defense Analyses) and James Hosek (RAND).

Abbreviations

AFQT	Armed Forces Qualification Test
AIT	Advanced Individual Training
AMSARA	Accession Medical Standards Analysis and Research Activity
ARMS	Assessment of Recruit Motivation and Strength
ATRRS	Army Training Requirements and Resources System
BCT	Basic Combat Training
BMI	body mass index
CMF	career management field
CRAN	Comprehensive R Archive Network
DEP	Delayed Entry Program
FY	fiscal year
GED	General Educational Development
GUI	graphical user interface
HQDA G-1	Headquarters Department of the Army, G-1 (Personnel)
IET	Initial Entry Training
MOS	military occupational specialty
OPAT	Occupational Physical Assessment Test
OSTAT	output status
OSUT	One Station Unit Training

PULHES	Physical capacity, Upper extremities, Lower extremities, Hearing, Eyes, and Psychiatric (0 to 4 health ratings)
RA	Regular (active) Army
RMC	Regular Military Compensation
RRM	Recruiting Resource Model
SPD	Separation Program Designator
TAPDB	Total Army Personnel Data Base
TTAS	Tier Two Attrition Screen

CHAPTER ONE

Introduction

Successful completion of the first term of enlistment is very important for both readiness and minimizing cost. Selecting recruits who do not complete their term is unnecessarily expensive and inefficient, because the Army is expending recruiting and Initial Entry Training (IET) resources on soldiers who must be replaced. Despite recent higher recruiting standards and a Future Soldier Training Program, the Army continues to experience its historical level of approximately 30–35 percent attrition over the first term. Policies to lower attrition often are based on a limited number of success predictors in isolation, such as having a traditional high school diploma or scoring in the upper half of the Armed Forces Qualification Test (AFQT) aptitude distribution (AFQT categories 1–3A), but research that considers how various factors work in combination is needed to develop more-successful recruit selection tools.

The research described in this report was requested by the Deputy Chief of Staff, G-1, and the Assistant Secretary of the Army, Manpower and Reserve Affairs. Its purpose is to provide the Army with a means of identifying the prospective effects of combinations of new recruits' cognitive, noncognitive, physical, demographic, and behavioral attributes on serving successfully and completing their first term, and on related costs, thus enabling the Army to identify potential changes to selection of youth based on these attributes in order to expand supply smartly or to decrease the rates of targeted adverse outcomes.

As described in the report, we accomplished this objective through a series of steps leading to development of a recruit selection tool for the

Army's use that accounts for the associations of various attributes, and their combinations, with soldier success; for potential compensatory factors; and for the costs of policy alternatives, including recruiting and training costs. This research can help the Army to minimize costs and maintain readiness by supporting recruits' first-term success, during periods of both force growth and reduction.

Chapter Two describes our research approach and initial phase of work. This included reviewing past research on the associations of demographic factors, waivers, qualification test scores, compensatory selection measures, physical condition, time between enlistment contract and accession (time in the Delayed Entry Program [DEP]), and term of service chosen with DEP, training, and first term attrition; adverse personnel actions (e.g., bar to reenlistment); and reasons for attrition. We then quantified the recent association of each enlistment characteristic identified in the literature separately with DEP, training, and first-term attrition outcomes, as well as the adverse personnel outcomes and reasons for separation. Next, using multivariate regression, we modeled the associations of the enlistment characteristics identified individually as the most important predictors with losses, the timing of those losses, adverse intermediate factors, and the reasons for separation when controlling for the other predictors. Regression results are provided in Chapter Two.

Using the factors found to be the primary drivers of the outcomes in the regression results, all else equal, we then built a tool to estimate the prospective effects on outcomes and the costs of making single or multiple changes in recruit cohort characteristics. The tool allows all of the natural covariation among recruit characteristics to affect the simulation of training performance, the level and timing of attrition, effects on adverse intermediate outcomes, and the rates and reasons for early separation. It quantifies recruiting, training, and replacement costs associated with these alternative combinations. Possible differences in compensation costs associated with these changes also are considered when the number of recruits with prior military service is changed. Using the tool, in Chapter Three and Appendix B we illustrate the prospective effects of simultaneous and single changes in three enlistment eligibility policy levers used historically by the Army to respond to changes in recruiting challenges—the percentage of education "Tier 2" recruits (primarily General Educational Development [GED] certificate holders),[1] the percentage of recruits with enlistment waivers, and the number of recruits with prior military service—on attrition, costs, and a broad range of other outcomes.

The recruit characteristics found to be the primary drivers of the outcomes in the regression results are all included in the tool database. The database covers every recruit into the Army during fiscal year (FY)01–FY11. It also contains the attrition, adverse outcome, reason for separation information, and related cost information discussed above, based on following these recruits into FY16. The user of the tool chooses the desired changes in recruit cohort characteristics. The tool then determines the weights to be applied to each soldier in the database to produce the new distribution of recruit characteristics based on the user's choices. It then averages over the weighted rows of soldiers to estimate the new cohort outcomes and costs.

Because we want all of the natural covariation among recruit characteristics to influence the behavioral and cost outcomes generated by the recruit selection tool, the regression results that hold all else equal are not directly used in the tool. However, the regression results provide important information in thinking about which characteristics to vary to achieve specific objectives and, in some cases, how to use the information concerning which specific factors are most highly associated with adverse outcomes for remediation.

Chapter Four reviews the research and results, and adds concluding thoughts. Supplemental statistical analyses are presented in Appendix A. Appendix B walks the reader through some illustrative uses of the tool. A user's guide explaining the use of the tool and the outputs it provides is presented in Appendix C.

---

1 Historically, Army practice has been to insist on greater AFQT category 1–3A levels among Tier 2 recruits. For this reason, as discussed in Chapter Three, the percentage of AFQT category 1–3As also is adjusted when the percentage of Tier 2 recruits is adjusted.

CHAPTER TWO

Research Approach for Initial Phase of Work

We began by reviewing past research concerning the associations of individual factors with DEP, IET, and first term attrition as well as relationships to intermediate factors related to negative outcomes (e.g., loss of favorable person status, reenlistment prohibition, demotion/negative rank change) and reasons for subsequent separation from the Army. The individual factors included demographic factors, education level and aptitude, medical and conduct waivers, prior military service, test scores, noncognitive/compensatory selection measures (e.g., Tier Two Attrition Screen [TTAS], Assessment of Recruit Motivation and Strength [ARMS]), body mass index (BMI), physical condition indicators, time in DEP, and enlistment contract length (term of service). The past research included a considerable body of work by the Army Research Institute on psychological screening measures for selection of new recruits with lower likelihoods of attrition; research by the RAND Corporation, the Army Research Institute, CNA's Center for Naval Analyses, the Naval Postgraduate School, the Army's Accession Medical Standards Analysis and Research Activity (AMSARA), and other institutions on the associations of demographic characteristics and routinely collected administrative information, such as test scores and physical characteristics with attrition and the reasons for it; and research by the Army Research Institute, AMSARA, and RAND on noncognitive and physical compensatory screening measures for identifying lower-risk youth among demand-constrained groups (GED holders and over-body-fat-limit candidates).[1]

[1] See the Bibliography for more-complete information on the past research reviewed.

Using enlistment contract information from the RA (Regular Army) Analyst files for FY01–FY11, records from the TAPDB (Total Army Personnel Data Base) Active Enlisted file for FY01–FY16, and information from the Army Training Requirements and Resources System for the same period, we next quantified the association of each enlistment characteristic identified in the literature separately with DEP, training, and first-term attrition. In addition to the associations of the individual enlistment characteristics with loss rates and the timing of the losses, we also examined the coded reasons for losses, and the relationships between the characteristics and adverse intermediate factors.

Using logistic regression analysis, we then modeled the joint associations of the enlistment characteristics identified individually as the most important predictors with losses, the timing of those losses (during the DEP, during training, or overall during the term), adverse intermediate factors, and the reasons for separation, controlling for recruits' levels on the other primary characteristics. The multivariate regression results for first-term performance (or contract term performance for recruits with prior service) are discussed below. Additional details are provided in Appendix A.

Regression Model Factors for DEP Survival and First-Term Performance

Based on our review of past research and our examination of the associations of the emerging factors with DEP, IET, and first-term attrition, their relationships to intermediate factors related to negative outcomes, and with the reasons for early separation from the Army, we included the factors listed in Table 2.1 in our regression analyses. For each recruit characteristic, the comparison group (omitted reference group

Table 2.1
Recruit Characteristics Included in Regression Analyses

Recruit Characteristic
Gender (male vs. female)
Age at enlistment contract (22–24, 25–30, 31–35, 36+ vs. 17–21)
Marital and children status (married, kids; married, no kids; formerly married, kids; formerly married, no kids; single, kids vs. single, no kids)
Race/ethnicity (Asian, African-American, Hispanic, other non-white non-Hispanic vs. white non-Hispanic)
Attended college (some college, graduated college vs. no college)
Enlistment waiver (traffic offense; non-traffic offense; drug/alcohol waiver; weight waiver; other health prior condition waiver when no PULHES measure = 3; other non-offense, non-health waiver vs. no waiver)
Months scheduled to be in the DEP
First term length (2 [DEP attrition only], 3, 5, 6 vs. 4 years)
Education tier (Tier 2 vs. Tier 1)
AFQT category (1–3A vs. 3B–4)
PULHES-related significant limitations (3 vs. <3)
BMI (each BMI decile vs. decile 5)
TTAS score (passed with 112 cutoff vs. did not pass)
ARMS score (passed vs. did not pass)
Prior military service (yes vs. no)
Contract/accession year (FY02–FY11 by year vs. FY01)
Contract/accession month (January–April, June–December vs. May)

NOTE: The DEP attrition analysis includes recruits who contracted in FY01–FY10; it excludes FY11 contracts because a significant number of such persons would be scheduled to access during FY12, outside of our accession window. The training and first-term attrition regressions include FY01–FY11 accessions; they exclude the two-year-term soldiers included in the DEP analysis because we want to focus on completing at least three years of service in the attrition analysis.

for characteristics with three or more subgroups) is indicated. For the most part, the characteristics are self-explanatory. For the others:

- "Months scheduled to be in the DEP" represents the time between when the recruit signed an enlistment contract and when he or she was due to report to initial training.
- "Education tier" refers to whether the recruit has a traditional high school diploma (or equivalent diploma by law or Office of the Secretary of Defense [OSD] policy) "Tier 1" or a GED (or equivalent diploma by law or OSD policy) "Tier 2."
- AFQT categories 1–3A indicate scores in the upper half of the national aptitude distribution, whereas categories 3B–4 reflect scores in the lower half.
- "PULHES-related significant limitations" refers to six areas of medical outcomes: physical capacity, upper extremities, lower extremities, hearing, eyes, and psychiatric.

Ratings in each area range from 1 (no limitations) to 4. Values of 3 or 4 indicate serious medical conditions and limitations, with a 4 generally making a youth ineligible for enlistment. BMI is based on one's weight relative to one's height. We divide the index values into deciles using the observed values over the entire data set, using decile 1 to represent the lowest ratio of weight to height and decile 10 to represent the highest ratio. TTAS is an assessment of motivation, BMI, and aptitude, developed by the Army Research Institute. The TTAS score was found to have a significant association with observed attrition rates over the first term of service when used to screen youth into the Army during the mid-2000s. (See, for example, Hunter, White, and Young, 2008). The cutoff score of 112 used in our analyses was designed to screen in the upper 30 percent of TTAS takers. ARMS was used by the Army during a similar period to screen in youth who were slightly over body fat limits but who passed this fitness test. ARMS consists of a five-minute step test and pushup test. (See Loughran and Orvis, 2011.)

Actual Outcome Rates for the Top Versus Bottom Quintiles of the Predicted Outcome Probabilities in the Regression Results

One indication of the utility of a regression model is the extent to which it distinguishes persons who are likely to do well on a given outcome from those who are likely do poorly. If we divide the predicted values for the enlistees in our database into five groups using their predicted scores on the outcome from the corresponding regression analysis, going from those predicted to do best to those predicted to do worst on the outcome, the question becomes the extent of the difference in the actual outcome rates for the top versus bottom groups. For the model to be useful and have predictive power, the actual rates for the outcome will be notably different between the two groups. A less useful model would have relatively similar actual rates for the outcome across all of the quintiles of its predicted values.

Table 2.2 shows the results of such an upper versus lower quintile comparison for selected key outcomes. As seen clearly in the table, the difference in the actual outcome rates for the top versus bottom groups is substantial: on the order of 20–30 percentage points for the failure-to-complete outcomes; 20–35 percentage points for the negative personnel flags; and 6–12 times as great a separation rate for each indicated reason, a difference of about 4 to 7 percentage points. (The ratio of the rates for separation due to parenthood/custody of minor children is much greater, but it is primarily gender-driven. The overall rates for each of these outcomes is relatively low because there is only one reason coded for a loss, and, together, across all of the codes shown in Table 2.2 and those not listed, the rates must sum to the first-term loss rate.)

Failure to Complete Delayed Entry Program, Initial Entry Training, or First Term

The results of our logistic regression analysis of failing to complete the DEP and, thus, not accessing onto active duty are shown in Table 2.3.

Table 2.2
Actual Outcome Rates for the Top Versus Bottom Quintiles of the Predicted Outcome Probabilities in Our Regression Results

Outcome
Failure to complete DEP (1.4% vs. 33.7%)
Failure to complete training (5.3% vs. 22.8%)
Failure to complete term (21.7% vs. 50.6%)
Negative personnel flag • Negative rank change (6.4% vs. 24.8%) • Bar to reenlistment (13.8% vs. 49.3%) • Suspension of favorable person status (30.0% vs. 66.7%)
Separation and reason • Separation due to parenthood/custody of minor children (0.1% vs. 4.4%) • Separation due to physical condition, not a disability (1.1% vs. 6.1%) • Separation due to failing medical/physical standard (0.7% vs. 7.3%) • Separation due to entry-level performance and conduct (0.6% vs. 7.4%) • Separation due to pattern of misconduct (0.5% vs. 4.0%) • Separation in lieu of trial by court-martial (0.4% vs. 4.6%) • Separation due to commission of a serious offense (0.6% vs. 4.1%) • Separation due to drug abuse (0.7% vs. 5.7%)

For ease of interpretation, we converted the odds ratios generated in the regression analysis to relative risk ratios, that is, the probability of failing to complete the DEP for a recruit with the indicated characteristic relative to that of a recruit with the opposite or reference group characteristic.[2] Given the very large number of observations, we focus only on differences of 10 percent or greater in the probability of a particular outcome and only when the probability of observing the difference by chance is less than one in 100,000. The means and standard deviations for the regressors are shown in Appendix A.

We find that a male recruit was only about half as likely to fail to complete the DEP as was a female recruit, other things equal. In

[2] The conversion is done by calculating the attrition rate for the reference group; substituting that rate into the odds ratio formula [i.e., (the probability of attrition for the specified group divided by one minus its probability of attrition) divided by (the probability of attrition for the reference group divided by one minus its probability of attrition)] and using the estimated odds ratio from the regression to derive the remaining probability for the specified group; and then taking the ratio of the attrition probabilities for the specified versus reference groups.

Table 2.3
Failure to Complete Delayed Entry Program
(N = 869,550; loss rate = 12.4 percent)

Variable	Observations	Risk Ratio	p
Male	710,863	0.535	0.00000
Age at contract 22–24	144,648	1.064	0.00000
Age at contract 25–30	110,731	1.166	0.00000
Age at contract 31–35	32,417	1.314	0.00000
Age at contract 36+	14,514	1.107	0.00185
Married, kids	107,542	1.171	0.00000
Married, no kids	56,077	0.172	0.00000
Formerly married, kids	9,410	1.067	0.05400
Formerly married, no kids	10,649	1.087	0.00323
Never married, kids	19,932	1.195	0.00000
Asian	27,014	0.901	0.00000
African-American	148,071	1.017	0.04530
Hispanic	92,217	1.012	0.24400
Other non-white non-Hispanic	14,232	0.932	0.00398
Some college	81,304	1.083	0.00000
Four-year college degree	38,735	0.924	0.00002
GED holder	126,200	2.430	0.00000
Traffic offense waiver	2,530	0.922	0.17900
Non-traffic offense waiver	53,505	0.927	0.00001
Drug/alcohol waiver	9,265	0.771	0.00000
Weight waiver	4,470	0.725	0.00000
Other health waiver	5,791	0.959	0.33500
Other non-health waiver	12,048	0.826	0.00000
Scheduled months in DEP	150,190	1.835	0.00000

Table 2.3—continued

Variable	Observations	Risk Ratio	p
Two-year enlistment	13,563	2.378	0.00000
Three-year enlistment	388,674	0.971	0.00014
Five-year enlistment	87,305	0.976	0.02120
Six-year enlistment	72,334	0.917	0.00000
AFQT categories 1–3A	572,729	0.884	0.00000
Physical capacity = 3	39,298	2.570	0.00000
Upper extremities = 3	6,387	1.924	0.00000
Lower extremities = 3	10,343	2.112	0.00000
Hearing = 3	6,054	1.156	0.00020
Vision = 3	10,641	1.089	0.00284
Psychiatric = 3	18,448	7.540	0.00000
BMI decile 1	81,981	1.191	0.00000
BMI decile 2	82,083	1.099	0.00000
BMI decile 3	82,065	1.074	0.00000
BMI decile 4	81,886	1.024	0.10900
BMI decile 6	81,638	0.961	0.00712
BMI decile 7	81,432	0.959	0.00533
BMI decile 8	81,614	0.972	0.06870
BMI decile 9	82,130	1.022	0.15600
BMI decile 10	81,210	1.189	0.00000
Passed TTAS 112 cutoff	21,422	0.915	0.74800
Took and passed ARMS	4,171	0.494	0.00000
Contract year FY02	99,012	0.594	0.00000
Contract year FY03	89,502	0.580	0.00000
Contract year FY04	73,497	0.501	0.00000
Contract year FY05	73,783	0.547	0.00000

Table 2.3—continued

Variable	Observations	Risk Ratio	p
Contract year FY06	89,368	0.478	0.00000
Contract year FY07	82,897	0.467	0.00000
Contract year FY08	91,035	0.445	0.00000
Contract year FY09	98,352	0.413	0.00000
Contract year FY10	85,826	0.820	0.00078
Contract month January	71,488	1.102	0.00000
Contract month February	67,870	1.080	0.00000
Contract month March	74,357	1.088	0.00000
Contract month April	70,478	1.052	0.00191
Contract month June	76,658	0.911	0.00000
Contract month July	77,055	0.918	0.00000
Contract month August	82,920	0.885	0.00000
Contract month September	79,249	0.882	0.00000
Contract month October	73,167	1.099	0.00000
Contract month November	64,424	1.112	0.00000
Contract month December	64,790	1.095	0.00000
Prior service	79,284	0.588	0.00000

contrast, recruits who were older were more likely to fail to complete the DEP than were recruits of ages 17–21. This was especially so for recruits in the ages 31–35 group, who were about 30 percent more likely to drop out of the DEP. Relative to recruits who had never been married and had no children, married recruits without children were much less likely to leave the DEP, whereas never married or married recruits with children were more likely to do so. Racial/ethnic differences in leaving the DEP were relatively small, as were those for recruits who had attended college relative to recruits who had not. In contrast, recruits who held GED degrees were nearly two-and-one-half times more likely to leave the DEP than recruits with traditional high school diplomas. Recruits with drug/alcohol, weight, or other non-health, non-legal-offense waivers were less likely to leave the DEP prematurely than were recruits without waivers. Loss rates from the DEP increased substantially with months scheduled in the DEP. Recruits who signed up for a two-year term were more than twice as likely to drop out of the DEP than were recruits enlisting for four-year terms of service (about the average term length chosen). Recruits in the upper half of the national aptitude distribution (AFQT categories 1–3A) were about 10 percent less likely to leave the DEP early than were those in the lower half. In contrast, recruits with serious limitations indicated for the physical capacity, upper extremities, or lower extremities PULHES assessments were twice as likely to fail to complete the DEP than those with fewer/no limitations, while those with serious psychiatric limitations were more than seven times as likely to fail to complete the DEP as were recruits without such limitations. Recruits who were very low weight for their height (BMI decile 1) or very high weight (BMI decile 10) were about 20 percent less likely to complete the DEP than were recruits of average weight for their height (BMI decile 5). Recruits who enlisted through the ARMS program were only half as likely to leave the DEP prematurely as were other recruits. Recruits enlisting after FY01 were less likely to leave the DEP early; there were no large differences by month of enlistment contract. Last, recruits with prior military service were only about 60 percent as likely to leave the DEP early as those without prior service, all else equal.

The results of our logistic regression analysis of failing to complete IET are shown in Table 2.4. We again focus only on differences when the probability of observing the difference by chance is less than one in 100,000. Similarly to the results for DEP losses, we find that a male recruit was only about half as likely to fail to complete initial training as was a female recruit, other things equal. In contrast, recruits who were over 30 were somewhat more likely to fail to complete the initial training than were recruits ages 17–21. Relative to recruits who had never been married and had no children, formerly married recruits were more likely to fail to complete initial training. Minority recruits were less likely to fail to complete initial training, as were recruits who had attended college relative to recruits who had not done so,

Table 2.4
Failure to Complete Initial Entry Training
(N = 688,211; loss rate = 12.6 percent)

Variable	Observations	Risk Ratio	p
Male	575,125	0.472	0.00000
Age at contract 22–24	110,510	0.897	0.00000
Age at contract 25–30	77,233	0.969	0.01310
Age at contract 31–35	22,037	1.144	0.00000
Age at contract 36+	9,903	1.123	0.00064
Married, kids	73,590	1.052	0.00002
Married, no kids	44,156	1.073	0.00000
Formerly married, kids	6,552	1.223	0.00000
Formerly married, no kids	7,394	1.164	0.00000
Never married, kids	15,651	1.070	0.00200
Asian	22,124	0.637	0.00000
African-American	116,585	0.715	0.00000
Hispanic	74,144	0.667	0.00000
Other non-white non-Hispanic	11,540	0.685	0.00000
Some college	64,219	0.888	0.00000
Four-year college degree	23,926	0.595	0.00000
GED holder	101,536	1.583	0.00000
Traffic offense waiver	2,107	0.676	0.00000
Non-traffic offense waiver	47,943	0.836	0.00000
Drug/alcohol waiver	8,272	0.965	0.24100
Weight waiver	3,825	1.003	0.93100
Other health waiver	5,386	1.156	0.00002
Other non-health waiver	9,521	0.997	0.88600
Scheduled months in DEP	120,189	0.905	0.00000

Table 2.4—continued

Variable	Observations	Risk Ratio	p
Three-year enlistment	293,138	0.921	0.00000
Five-year enlistment	72,426	0.935	0.00000
Six-year enlistment	62,779	1.115	0.00000
AFQT categories 1–3A	448,443	0.946	0.00000
Physical capacity = 3	25,206	1.228	0.00000
Upper extremities = 3	4,522	1.218	0.00000
Lower extremities = 3	6,754	1.594	0.00000
Hearing = 3	4,558	1.059	0.15400
Vision = 3	8,403	1.138	0.00000
Psychiatric = 3	5,999	1.597	0.00000
BMI decile 1	64,905	1.123	0.00000
BMI decile 2	66,085	1.014	0.35200
BMI decile 3	65,834	0.982	0.23500
BMI decile 4	65,660	0.994	0.68800
BMI decile 6	65,200	1.033	0.03010
BMI decile 7	64,908	1.061	0.00012
BMI decile 8	65,696	1.108	0.00000
BMI decile 9	66,714	1.210	0.00000
BMI decile 10	67,157	1.415	0.00000
Passed TTAS 112 cutoff	20,462	0.770	0.00000
Took and passed ARMS	3,560	0.833	0.00002
Accession year FY02	63,353	2.324	0.00000
Accession year FY03	61,819	2.524	0.00000
Accession year FY04	67,724	2.887	0.00000
Accession year FY05	58,914	2.091	0.00000
Accession year FY06	67,577	1.526	0.00000

Table 2.4—continued

Variable	Observations	Risk Ratio	p
Accession year FY07	65,708	1.929	0.00000
Accession year FY08	67,600	2.079	0.00000
Accession year FY09	61,203	2.215	0.00000
Accession year FY10	67,661	2.145	0.00000
Accession year FY11	52,753	2.068	0.00000
Accession month January	78,688	0.952	0.00158
Accession month February	54,465	0.987	0.42800
Accession month March	52,936	1.009	0.58500
Accession month April	51,119	1.009	0.61900
Accession month June	69,279	0.979	0.18700
Accession month July	73,348	0.931	0.00002
Accession month August	77,125	0.975	0.11600
Accession month September	59,049	1.061	0.00017
Accession month October	61,626	1.103	0.00000
Accession month November	50,448	1.235	0.00000
Accession month December	8,618	1.061	0.06080
Prior service	35,431	0.345	0.00000

NOTE: Approximately 13.5 percent of the accessions included in next table lacked verifiable training data and were therefore excluded from this analysis.

especially those with four-year degrees. In contrast, recruits who held GED degrees were more than one-and-one-half times as likely not to complete training as recruits with traditional high school diplomas. Recruits with traffic offense or non-traffic offense waivers were substantially less likely to fail to complete training, whereas those with non-weight health waivers were about 15 percent more likely to do so. The differences across scheduled time in the DEP, terms of enlistment, or AFQT category were not large, though the result for months in the DEP is multiplicative, so differences of more than one month were associated with different training outcomes. Recruits with serious limitations indicated for the physical capacity, upper extremities, and, especially lower extremities or psychiatric PULHES assessments were more likely to fail to complete initial training than those with fewer/no limitations. Similarly, recruits who were substantially over average weight (BMI deciles 9 and 10) were, respectively, about 20 percent and 40 percent more likely to fail to complete initial training than were recruits of average weight for their height (BMI decile 5). Recruits who scored in the top 30 percentiles of the TTAS distribution (score of 112 or higher) or who accessed through the ARMS program were less likely to fail to complete initial training. Recruits accessing after FY01 were more likely to fail to complete initial training, perhaps because they were less likely leave the DEP early (i.e., losses became more even over time); there are no large differences by month of accession except for higher training losses for November accessions, which might be at least partly associated with breaks over the Christmas holiday. Last, recruits with prior military service were only about one-third as likely to fail to complete initial training as those without prior service, all else equal.

The results of our logistic regression analysis of failing to complete one's term of service are shown in Table 2.5. Failure in this analysis is defined as serving less than three years for a three-year enlistment or less than four years for a term of four years or longer. Enlistees for two-year terms are excluded. Similarly to the results for DEP and IET losses, we find that a male recruit was much less likely to fail to complete his first term than was a female recruit, other things equal. Similarly, recruits who were over 21 years of age at enlistment—especially those 36 years of age or older—were somewhat less likely to fail to complete their first term than were recruits ages 17–21. Relative to recruits who had never been married and had no children, formerly married recruits were more likely to fail to complete their first term. In contrast, minority recruits were less likely to fail to complete their first term. Recruits with four-year college degrees were more likely to leave early; additional analysis shows that this difference was associated with becoming officers. Recruits who held GED degrees were about 40 percent more likely not to complete their first term than were recruits with traditional high school diplomas. Similarly, recruits with drug/

Table 2.5
Failure to Complete Term of Service (N = 795,940; loss rate = 34.5 percent)

Variable	Observations	Risk Ratio	p
Male	663,365	0.611	0.00000
Age at contract 22–24	135,629	0.900	0.00000
Age at contract 25–30	103,799	0.885	0.00000
Age at contract 31–35	29,824	0.875	0.00000
Age at contract 36+	13,733	0.739	0.00000
Married, kids	98,481	1.036	0.00000
Married, no kids	57,760	1.031	0.00000
Formerly married, kids	8,551	1.236	0.00000
Formerly married, no kids	9,758	1.206	0.00000
Never married, kids	17,974	1.125	0.00000
Asian	25,318	0.703	0.00000
African-American	136,340	0.878	0.00000
Hispanic	84,668	0.758	0.00000
Other non-white non-Hispanic	12,955	0.801	0.00000
Some college	73,113	0.984	0.00807
Four-year college degree	37,339	1.551	0.00000
GED holder	114,107	1.416	0.00000
Traffic offense waiver	2,184	0.949	0.09130
Non-traffic offense waiver	49,507	1.066	0.00000
Drug/alcohol waiver	8,548	1.339	0.00000
Weight waiver	4,002	1.025	0.24700
Other health waiver	5,741	1.067	0.00033
Other non-health waiver	11,345	1.137	0.00000
Scheduled months in DEP	138,656	0.998	0.01010
Three-year enlistment	367,583	0.867	0.00000

Table 2.5—continued

Variable	Observations	Risk Ratio	p
Five-year enlistment	80,166	0.922	0.00000
Six-year enlistment	68,620	0.945	0.00000
AFQT categories 1–3A	520,088	0.949	0.00000
Physical capacity = 3	29,541	1.101	0.00000
Upper extremities = 3	5,240	1.097	0.00000
Lower extremities = 3	8,114	1.273	0.00000
Hearing = 3	5,522	1.071	0.00047
Vision = 3	10,055	1.065	0.00000
Psychiatric = 3	6,929	1.421	0.00000
BMI decile 1	72,308	1.038	0.00000
BMI decile 2	73,896	1.008	0.26200
BMI decile 3	74,347	0.990	0.18200
BMI decile 4	74,862	0.993	0.37600
BMI decile 6	75,990	1.007	0.32200
BMI decile 7	76,351	1.018	0.01700
BMI decile 8	76,793	1.039	0.00000
BMI decile 9	77,079	1.078	0.00000
BMI decile 10	75,361	1.213	0.00000
Passed TTAS 112 cutoff	21,344	0.906	0.00000
Took and passed ARMS	3,785	0.955	0.03480
Accession year FY02	74,017	1.116	0.00000
Accession year FY03	70,500	1.095	0.00000
Accession year FY04	77,449	1.104	0.00000
Accession year FY05	68,993	0.997	0.73800
Accession year FY06	78,247	0.902	0.00000
Accession year FY07	78,575	0.936	0.00000

Table 2.5—continued

Variable	Observations	Risk Ratio	p
Accession year FY08	79,070	0.974	0.00095
Accession year FY09	68,293	1.013	0.12700
Accession year FY10	73,841	0.999	0.90000
Accession year FY11	63,268	1.247	0.00000
Accession month January	89,715	0.978	0.00322
Accession month February	65,142	1.089	0.00000
Accession month March	61,568	1.048	0.00000
Accession month April	60,434	1.008	0.32800
Accession month June	80,268	1.007	0.35400
Accession month July	84,261	0.973	0.00066
Accession month August	85,980	0.972	0.00026
Accession month September	66,804	1.007	0.37700
Accession month October	71,435	1.042	0.00000
Accession month November	57,828	1.069	0.00000
Accession month December	13,069	0.973	0.07670
Prior service	76,013	0.749	0.00000

alcohol waivers were about one-third more likely to fail to complete their first term than those without enlistment waivers, and those with "other non-health" waivers were about 15 percent more likely to fail to do so. The differences across scheduled time in the DEP, terms of enlistment, or AFQT category were not large; three-year enlistees were about 10–15 percent less likely to leave early than four-year enlistees, perhaps because of the shorter obligation. In contrast, recruits with serious limitations indicated for the lower extremities or psychiatric PULHES assessments were more likely to fail to complete their first term than those with fewer/no limitations. Recruits who were well over average weight (BMI decile 10) were about 20 percent more likely to fail to complete their first term than were recruits of average weight for their height (BMI decile 5). Recruits accessing in FY11 were more likely to fail to complete their first term; there were no large differences by month of accession. Last, recruits with prior military service were only about 75 percent as likely to fail to complete their term of enlistment as those without prior service, all else equal.

Table 2.6 summarizes our primary attrition results for recruit characteristics. Given the very large number of observations, here, for the primary effects, we focus only on differences of 20 percent or greater in the probability of attrition and only when the probability of observing the difference by chance is less than one in 100,000. The plus or minus signs show the direction of the association with attrition. We note that the results are generally consistent with the associations found for the included characteristics in the earlier research referenced previously. One of the most direct comparisons is with Buddin (2005), who also included DEP, training, and first-term attrition in his study. The results for BMI and health waivers are similarly consistent with results found by Niebuhr et al. (2009).

Negative Personnel Flags

We examined three types of adverse personnel actions that can be experienced by recruits during their term of service: rank reduction, bar to reenlistment, and suspension of favorable person status; they apply to about 15 percent, 30 percent, and 50 percent of enlistees, respectively. We discuss the results for the two more serious personnel actions: a rank reduction and a bar to reenlistment.

The results of our logistic regression analysis of experiencing a negative change (punitive reduction) in one's rank are shown in Table 2.7. We find that a male recruit was about 40 percent more likely to experience a rank reduction than was a female recruit, other things equal. In contrast, older recruits were considerably less likely to experience a rank reduction than recruits of ages 17–21, and the magnitude of the difference increased with the recruit's age. Relative to recruits who had never been married and had no children, married recruits were less likely to experience a rank reduction. The effects for minority recruits varied:

Table 2.6
Summary of Attrition Results

Variable	DEP Loss	IET Loss	First Term Loss
Male	–	–	–
Age at contract 22–24			
Age at contract 25–30			
Age at contract 31–35	–		
Age at contract 36+			–
Married, kids			
Married, no kids			
Formerly married, kids		+	+
Formerly married, no kids			+
Never married, kids			
Asian		–	–
African-American		–	
Hispanic		–	–
Other non-white non-Hispanic		–	–
Some college			
Four-year college degree		–	+
GED holder	+	+	+
Traffic offense waiver		–	
Non-traffic offense waiver			
Drug/alcohol waiver	–		+
Weight waiver	–		
Other health waiver			
Other non-health waiver			
Scheduled months in DEP	+		

Table 2.6—continued

Variable	DEP Loss	IET Loss	First Term Loss
Two-year enlistment	+	N/A	N/A
Three-year enlistment			
Five-year enlistment			
Six-year enlistment			
AFQT categories 1–3A			
Physical capacity = 3	+	+	
Upper extremities = 3	+	+	
Lower extremities = 3	+	+	+
Hearing = 3			
Vision = 3			
Psychiatric = 3	+	+	+
BMI decile 1			
BMI decile 2			
BMI decile 3			
BMI decile 4			
BMI decile 6			
BMI decile 7			
BMI decile 8			
BMI decile 9		+	
BMI decile 10		+	+
Passed TTAS 112 cutoff		–	
Took and passed ARMS	–		
Prior service	–	–	–

Table 2.7
Rank Reduction (N = 795,940; rank reduction rate = 14.6 percent)

Variable	Observations	Risk Ratio	p
Male	663,365	1.433	0.00000
Age at contract 22–24	135,629	0.741	0.00000
Age at contract 25–30	103,799	0.640	0.00000
Age at contract 31–35	29,824	0.532	0.00000
Age at contract 36+	13,733	0.387	0.00000
Married, kids	98,481	0.767	0.00000
Married, no kids	57,760	0.780	0.00000
Formerly married, kids	8,551	1.031	0.32500
Formerly married, no kids	9,758	0.925	0.01220
Never married, kids	17,974	1.032	0.06410
Asian	25,318	0.797	0.00000
African-American	136,340	1.569	0.00000
Hispanic	84,668	0.999	0.91300
Other non-white non-Hispanic	12,955	1.192	0.00000
Some college	73,113	0.784	0.00000
Four-year college degree	37,339	0.443	0.00000
GED holder	114,107	1.353	0.00000
Traffic offense waiver	2,184	1.638	0.00000
Non-traffic offense waiver	49,507	1.527	0.00000
Drug/alcohol waiver	8,548	1.938	0.00000
Weight waiver	4,002	1.003	0.94000
Other health waiver	5,741	0.997	0.91000
Other non-health waiver	11,345	0.933	0.02750
Scheduled months in DEP	138,656	0.915	0.00000
Three-year enlistment	367,583	0.816	0.00000

Table 2.7—continued

Variable	Observations	Risk Ratio	p
Five-year enlistment	80,166	0.910	0.00000
Six-year enlistment	68,620	0.970	0.00392
AFQT categories 1–3A	520,088	0.879	0.00000
Physical capacity = 3	29,541	0.901	0.00000
Upper extremities = 3	5,240	0.967	0.35600
Lower extremities = 3	8,114	0.894	0.00028
Hearing = 3	5,522	1.024	0.49500
Vision = 3	10,055	0.907	0.00073
Psychiatric = 3	6,929	1.092	0.00227
BMI decile 1	72,308	1.023	0.06210
BMI decile 2	73,896	1.068	0.00000
BMI decile 3	74,347	1.028	0.02580
BMI decile 4	74,862	1.030	0.01640
BMI decile 6	75,990	0.971	0.02130
BMI decile 7	76,351	0.920	0.00000
BMI decile 8	76,793	0.910	0.00000
BMI decile 9	77,079	0.912	0.00000
BMI decile 10	75,361	0.858	0.00000
Passed TTAS 112 cutoff	21,344	1.086	0.00000
Took and passed ARMS	3,785	1.127	0.00235
Accession year FY02	74,017	0.861	0.00000
Accession year FY03	70,500	0.936	0.00000
Accession year FY04	77,449	0.985	0.28400
Accession year FY05	68,993	1.084	0.00000
Accession year FY06	78,247	1.134	0.00000
Accession year FY07	78,575	1.155	0.00000

Table 2.7—continued

Variable	Observations	Risk Ratio	p
Accession year FY08	79,070	1.148	0.00000
Accession year FY09	68,293	1.088	0.00000
Accession year FY10	73,841	1.043	0.00379
Accession year FY11	63,268	0.971	0.05790
Accession month January	89,715	1.003	0.83400
Accession month February	65,142	1.002	0.90400
Accession month March	61,568	1.020	0.15600
Accession month April	60,434	1.023	0.11500
Accession month June	80,268	1.048	0.00052
Accession month July	84,261	1.031	0.02180
Accession month August	85,980	0.986	0.31000
Accession month September	66,804	0.959	0.00290
Accession month October	71,435	0.978	0.10800
Accession month November	57,828	0.979	0.13300
Accession month December	13,069	1.060	0.01600
Prior service	76,013	1.376	0.00000

Asians were less likely to experience a rank reduction relative to white, non-Hispanic recruits, whereas African-American recruits and Other minority recruits were about 50 percent and 20 percent more likely to experience one, respectively. Recruits who had attended college were less likely to experience a rank reduction relative to recruits who had not done so, whereas recruits who held GED degrees were about one-third more likely to experience one than were recruits with traditional high school diplomas.[3] Recruits with traffic offense or non-traffic

[3] We would note that lower rates of adverse personnel flags for recruits with four years of college are likely at least partially attributable to their greater departure rate during their term to become officers.

offense waivers or drug/alcohol waivers were substantially more likely to experience a rank reduction. The difference across scheduled time in the DEP was notable, with the likelihood of a rank reduction decreasing substantially with two or more months spent in the DEP, perhaps due to attrition among recruits experiencing early problems. Recruits enlisting for three-year terms of service were about 20 percent less likely to experience a rank reduction than four-year enlistees, perhaps due to less exposure over time. Recruits in AFQT categories 1–3A were about 10 percent less likely to experience rank reductions than recruits with lower aptitude. Rank reduction rates for recruits with serious limitations indicated on PULHES indicators did not differ substantially from those for recruits with fewer/no limitations. BMI was not a big factor in rank reductions either, with the exception that recruits who were very high weight for their height (BMI decile 10) were about 15 percent less likely to experience one than recruits of average weight for their height (BMI decile 5). Relative to recruits who accessed in FY01, recruits accessing in FY02 were about 15 percent less likely to experience a rank reduction, whereas those accessing during FY06–FY08 were about 15 percent more likely to experience one. FY06–FY08 was a very difficult recruiting period; the increase in rank reductions for recruits accessed during that period could be associated with reduction in enlistment propensity due to the very low unemployment rate and the related, substantial increases in incentives and enlistment eligibility during FY06–FY08. There were no large differences in rank reductions by month of accession. Last, recruits with prior military service were about one-third more likely to experience a rank reduction than those without prior service, all else equal.

The results of our logistic regression analysis of experiencing a bar to reenlistment are shown in Table 2.8. We found little difference by gender in the likelihood of experiencing a bar to reenlistment, other things equal. In contrast, older recruits were considerably less likely to experience a bar to reenlistment than were recruits of ages 17–21, and the magnitude of the difference increased with the recruit's age. There was little difference in the likelihood of experiencing a bar to reenlistment by marital or child status. African-American recruits and "Other" minority recruits were about 15 percent more likely to experience one.

Table 2.8
Bar to Reenlistment (N = 795,940; bar to reenlistment rate = 29.4 percent)

Variable	Observations	Risk Ratio	p
Male	663,365	1.027	0.00000
Age at contract 22–24	135,629	0.913	0.00000
Age at contract 25–30	103,799	0.867	0.00000
Age at contract 31–35	29,824	0.796	0.00000
Age at contract 36+	13,733	0.720	0.00000
Married, kids	98,481	0.929	0.00000
Married, no kids	57,760	0.916	0.00000
Formerly married, kids	8,551	1.019	0.32200
Formerly married, no kids	9,758	0.954	0.00949
Never married, kids	17,974	1.010	0.43200
Asian	25,318	0.964	0.00146
African-American	136,340	1.155	0.00000
Hispanic	84,668	1.038	0.00000
Other non-white non-Hispanic	12,955	1.161	0.00000
Some college	73,113	0.829	0.00000
Four-year college degree	37,339	0.509	0.00000
GED holder	114,107	1.109	0.00000
Traffic offense waiver	2,184	1.099	0.02320
Non-traffic offense waiver	49,507	1.113	0.00000
Drug/alcohol waiver	8,548	1.219	0.00000
Weight waiver	4,002	1.166	0.00000
Other health waiver	5,741	1.007	0.68200
Other non-health waiver	11,345	0.922	0.00000
Scheduled months in DEP	138,656	0.976	0.00000

Table 2.8—continued

Variable	Observations	Risk Ratio	p
Three-year enlistment	367,583	0.840	0.00000
Five-year enlistment	80,166	0.823	0.00000
Six-year enlistment	68,620	0.800	0.00000
AFQT categories 1–3A	520,088	0.920	0.00000
Physical capacity = 3	29,541	0.981	0.04590
Upper extremities = 3	5,240	0.962	0.09230
Lower extremities = 3	8,114	0.955	0.01380
Hearing = 3	5,522	1.135	0.00000
Vision = 3	10,055	1.042	0.01200
Psychiatric = 3	6,929	0.952	0.01670
BMI decile 1	72,308	0.880	0.00000
BMI decile 2	73,896	0.899	0.00000
BMI decile 3	74,347	0.925	0.00000
BMI decile 4	74,862	0.938	0.00000
BMI decile 6	75,990	1.051	0.00000
BMI decile 7	76,351	1.140	0.00000
BMI decile 8	76,793	1.292	0.00000
BMI decile 9	77,079	1.471	0.00000
BMI decile 10	75,361	1.741	0.00000
Passed TTAS 112 cutoff	21,344	1.039	0.00608
Took and passed ARMS	3,785	1.153	0.00000
Accession year FY02	74,017	0.869	0.00000
Accession year FY03	70,500	0.735	0.00000
Accession year FY04	77,449	0.593	0.00000
Accession year FY05	68,993	0.539	0.00000

Table 2.8—continued

Variable	Observations	Risk Ratio	p
Accession year FY06	78,247	0.570	0.00000
Accession year FY07	78,575	0.759	0.00000
Accession year FY08	79,070	1.019	0.01970
Accession year FY09	68,293	1.241	0.00000
Accession year FY10	73,841	1.487	0.00000
Accession year FY11	63,268	1.649	0.00000
Accession month January	89,715	0.962	0.00001
Accession month February	65,142	0.974	0.00410
Accession month March	61,568	0.977	0.01010
Accession month April	60,434	0.996	0.66300
Accession month June	80,268	1.033	0.00032
Accession month July	84,261	1.035	0.00011
Accession month August	85,980	1.016	0.08240
Accession month September	66,804	1.005	0.58400
Accession month October	71,435	0.941	0.00000
Accession month November	57,828	0.932	0.00000
Accession month December	13,069	0.995	0.75800
Prior service	76,013	1.384	0.00000

Recruits who had attended college were less likely to experience a bar to reenlistment relative to recruits who had not done so, and especially so for those with four-year degrees (who were more likely to leave early to become officers, as noted earlier). Recruits who held GED degrees were about 10 percent more likely to experience a bar to reenlistment than were recruits with traditional high school diplomas. Similarly, recruits with non-traffic offense waivers, drug/alcohol waivers, or weight waivers were 10–20 percent more likely to experience a bar to reenlistment. The difference across scheduled time in the DEP was limited.

Recruits enlisting for terms of service other than four years were about 15–20 percent less likely to experience a bar to reenlistment.[4] There were limited differences in the likelihood of a reenlistment bar for recruits in AFQT categories 1–3A versus recruits with lower aptitude, and, for the most part, for recruits with serious limitations indicated on PULHES indicators relative to those for recruits with fewer/no limitations. The exception was that recruits with serious hearing limitations were about 10–15 percent more likely to experience a bar to reenlistment. Recruits in the lowest BMI deciles were about 10 percent less likely to experience a bar to reenlistment, whereas recruits who were over average weight (BMI deciles 7–10) were about 15–75 percent more likely to experience one; the likelihood increased substantially with each decile above decile 7. Analogously, recruits who accessed through the ARMS program due to being over body fat limits were 15 percent more likely to experience a bar to reenlistment. Relative to recruits who accessed in FY01, recruits accessing in FY02–FY07 were much less likely to experience a bar to reenlistment, whereas those accessing during FY09–FY11 were more likely to experience one. Related to the point discussed earlier, the early period coincides with a time of increasing and extreme recruiting difficulty, whereas the unemployment rate was increasing by FY09 and recruiting became much easier afterward. Since end strength is maintained by a combination of recruiting and retention efforts, the differences in reenlistment bar rates for recruits could be associated with the stress on recruiting, decreasing when recruiting is tough and increasing when it is much easier. There were no large differences in bars to reenlistment by month of accession. Last, recruits with prior military service were about one-third more likely to experience a reenlistment bar than those without prior service, all else equal.

Table 2.9 summarizes our primary results for demotions and bars to reenlistment. As noted for Table 2.6, given the very large number of observations, here, for the primary effects, we focus only on differences of 20 percent or greater in the probability of the adverse outcome and only when the probability of observing the difference by chance is less

---

4 The reason for this difference is not clear, though it could be related to term length (three years) and occupational specialty (five and six years).

Table 2.9
Summary of Adverse Personnel Flag Results

Variable	Rank Reduction	Bar to Reenlistment
Male	+	
Age at contract 22–24	–	
Age at contract 25–30	–	
Age at contract 31–35	–	–
Age at contract 36+	–	–
Married, kids	–	
Married, no kids	–	
Formerly married, kids		
Formerly married, no kids		
Never married, kids		
Asian	–	
African-American	+	
Hispanic		
Other non-white non-Hispanic		
Some college	–	
Four-year college degree	–	–
GED holder	+	
Traffic offense waiver	+	
Non-traffic offense waiver	+	
Drug/alcohol waiver	+	+
Weight waiver		
Other health waiver		
Other non-health waiver		
Scheduled months in DEP		
Three-year enlistment		

Table 2.9—continued

Variable	Rank Reduction	Bar to Reenlistment
Five-year enlistment		
Six-year enlistment		–
AFQT categories 1–3A		
Physical capacity = 3		+
Upper extremities = 3		+
Lower extremities = 3		+
Hearing = 3		
Vision = 3		
Psychiatric = 3		+
BMI decile 1		
BMI decile 2		
BMI decile 3		
BMI decile 4		
BMI decile 6		
BMI decile 7		
BMI decile 8		+
BMI decile 9		+
BMI decile 10		+
Passed TTAS 112 cutoff		
Took and passed ARMS		
Prior service	+	+

than one in 100,000. The plus or minus signs show the direction of the association with the adverse outcome.

Reasons for Separation

We focus next on the rates of experiencing early separations for various reasons coded by the Army in its Separation Program Designator variable found in the TAPDB. As before, given the very large number of observations, we focus only on differences of 10 percent or greater in the probability of a particular outcome and only when the probability of observing the difference by chance is less than one in 100,000. We also focus only on reasons for separation that represent at least 2 percent of the recruits. The results of our logistic regression analysis of experiencing a separation for entry-level performance and conduct are shown in Table 2.10. Such separations may occur while the solider is in entry-level status (training, typically six months) if a soldier is unqualified for further military service due to unsatisfactory performance, conduct, or both. We find that a male recruit was about half as likely to experience such an early separation than a female recruit, other things equal. Analogously, recruits 22–30 years of age were about 15–20 percent less likely to experience a separation for entry-level performance and conduct than were recruits of ages 17–21. Minority recruits were 15–30 percent less likely to experience a separation for entry-level performance and conduct relative to white, non-Hispanic recruits. Recruits who had four-year college degrees were about 40 percent less likely to experience a separation for entry-level performance and conduct, whereas recruits who held GED degrees were about 50 percent more likely to experience one than were recruits with traditional high school diplomas. Recruits with traffic offense or non-traffic offense waivers were 20–40 percent less likely to experience a separation for entry-level performance and conduct than were recruits without waivers, whereas those with waivers for a prior health condition not involving serious limitations indicated on a PULHES measure were 30 percent more likely to experience one ($p < .00001$). The difference across scheduled months in the DEP was notable, with the likelihood of a separation

Table 2.10
Separation for Entry-Level Performance and Conduct
(N = 795,940; separation rate for entry-level performance and conduct = 3.3 percent)

Variable	Observations	Risk Ratio	p
Male	663,365	0.458	0.00000
Age at contract 22–24	135,629	0.812	0.00000
Age at contract 25–30	103,799	0.840	0.00000
Age at contract 31–35	29,824	0.967	0.41100
Age at contract 36+	13,733	0.994	0.93800
Married, kids	98,481	1.029	0.22200
Married, no kids	57,760	1.044	0.08720
Formerly married, kids	8,551	1.082	0.26000
Formerly married, no kids	9,758	1.241	0.00011
Never married, kids	17,974	1.056	0.18900
Asian	25,318	0.826	0.00000
African-American	136,340	0.849	0.00000
Hispanic	84,668	0.771	0.00000
Other non-white non-Hispanic	12,955	0.716	0.00000
Some college	73,113	0.931	0.00158
Four-year college degree	37,339	0.585	0.00000
GED holder	114,107	1.485	0.00000
Traffic offense waiver	2,184	0.608	0.00006
Non-traffic offense waiver	49,507	0.827	0.00000
Drug/alcohol waiver	8,548	0.871	0.02870
Weight waiver	4,002	0.990	0.90800
Other health waiver	5,741	1.311	0.00001
Other non-health waiver	11,345	1.008	0.87800

Table 2.10—continued

Variable	Observations	Risk Ratio	p
Scheduled months in DEP	138,656	0.918	0.00000
Three-year enlistment	367,583	0.963	0.01170
Five-year enlistment	80,166	0.765	0.00000
Six-year enlistment	68,620	0.977	0.30800
AFQT categories 1–3A	520,088	0.799	0.00000
Physical capacity = 3	29,541	1.074	0.02290
Upper extremities = 3	5,240	0.649	0.00001
Lower extremities = 3	8,114	0.854	0.01980
Hearing = 3	5,522	1.136	0.08460
Vision = 3	10,055	1.157	0.00563
Psychiatric = 3	6,929	1.925	0.00000
BMI decile 1	72,308	1.110	0.00020
BMI decile 2	73,896	0.985	0.62000
BMI decile 3	74,347	0.943	0.04650
BMI decile 4	74,862	0.978	0.43900
BMI decile 6	75,990	1.074	0.01310
BMI decile 7	76,351	1.150	0.00000
BMI decile 8	76,793	1.268	0.00000
BMI decile 9	77,079	1.349	0.00000
BMI decile 10	75,361	1.711	0.00000
Passed TTAS 112 cutoff	21,344	0.713	0.00000
Took and passed ARMS	3,785	0.711	0.00518
Accession year FY02	74,017	4.356	0.00000
Accession year FY03	70,500	3.861	0.00000
Accession year FY04	77,449	4.917	0.00000

Table 2.10—continued

Variable	Observations	Risk Ratio	p
Accession year FY05	68,993	2.326	0.00000
Accession year FY06	78,247	0.763	0.00000
Accession year FY07	78,575	1.159	0.00147
Accession year FY08	79,070	1.612	0.00000
Accession year FY09	68,293	2.558	0.00000
Accession year FY10	73,841	3.777	0.00000
Accession year FY11	63,268	3.217	0.00000
Accession month January	89,715	0.942	0.03770
Accession month February	65,142	0.972	0.35500
Accession month March	61,568	1.014	0.65300
Accession month April	60,434	1.022	0.46700
Accession month June	80,268	0.952	0.11300
Accession month July	84,261	0.855	0.00000
Accession month August	85,980	1.018	0.53100
Accession month September	66,804	1.065	0.03760
Accession month October	71,435	1.072	0.01640
Accession month November	57,828	1.256	0.00000
Accession month December	13,069	0.742	0.00001
Prior service	76,013	0.090	0.00000

for entry-level performance and conduct decreasing with more time spent in the DEP, perhaps due to attrition among recruits experiencing early problems. Recruits enlisting for five-year terms of service were about 25 percent less likely to experience a separation for entry-level performance and conduct than four-year enlistees. The reason for this difference is not clear; it could possibly be related to the occupational specialties for which five-year terms were common during the study period. Recruits in AFQT categories 1–3A were about 20 percent less likely to experience a separation for entry-level performance and conduct than recruits with lower aptitude. A separation for entry-level performance and conduct was about one-third less likely for recruits with serious limitations indicated on the upper extremities PULHES measure than for recruits with fewer/no limitations on that measure ($p < .00001$); however, recruits with serious limitations indicated on the psychiatric PULHES measure were nearly twice as likely to experience a separation for entry-level performance and conduct than were recruits with fewer/no limitations on the psychiatric measure. Recruits who were above average weight for their height (BMI deciles 7–10) were about 15–70 percent more likely to experience a separation for entry-level performance and conduct than were recruits of average weight for their height (BMI decile 5); the risk increased with BMI. Recruits who scored 112 or better on the TTAS test were about 30 percent less likely to separate for entry-level performance and conduct than were recruits who scored lower. Relative to recruits who accessed in FY01, recruits accessing in later years were more likely to experience a separation for entry-level performance and conduct, except for FY06–FY07 recruits (perhaps due to the great recruiting difficulty during this period). There were limited differences in the rates of separation for entry-level performance and conduct by month of accession; the rate for July recruits, disproportionately graduating high school seniors, was about 15 percent lower than for May accessions, and the rate for the limited number of December accessions was about 25 percent lower ($p < .00001$). In contrast, the rate for November accessions was about 25 percent higher. Last, recruits with prior military service were only about 10 percent as likely to experience a separation for entry-level performance and conduct as those without prior service, all else equal. This difference was likely due in part to the fact that most prior-service recruits do not need to repeat IET.

The results of our logistic regression analysis of experiencing a separation due to a physical condition other than a disability are shown in Table 2.11. Such separations can occur when a soldier's physical performance or mental condition worsens or adversely effects other unit members. We found that a male recruit was about half as likely to

Table 2.11
Separation for a Physical Condition Other Than a Disability (N = 795,940; separation rate for physical condition other than a disability = 3.1 percent)

Variable	Observations	Risk Ratio	p
Male	663,365	0.500	0.00000
Age at contract 22–24	135,629	0.908	0.00000
Age at contract 25–30	103,799	0.930	0.00304
Age at contract 31–35	29,824	1.036	0.38800
Age at contract 36+	13,733	1.052	0.38800
Married, kids	98,481	0.906	0.00006
Married, no kids	57,760	1.059	0.02280
Formerly married, kids	8,551	1.157	0.02060
Formerly married, no kids	9,758	1.189	0.00151
Never married, kids	17,974	0.927	0.10700
Asian	25,318	0.689	0.00000
African-American	136,340	0.491	0.00000
Hispanic	84,668	0.644	0.00000
Other non-white non-Hispanic	12,955	0.598	0.00000
Some college	73,113	0.916	0.00025
Four-year college degree	37,339	0.670	0.00000
GED holder	114,107	1.262	0.00000
Traffic offense waiver	2,184	0.834	0.17900
Non-traffic offense waiver	49,507	0.826	0.00000
Drug/alcohol waiver	8,548	0.753	0.00014
Weight waiver	4,002	1.091	0.25500
Other health waiver	5,741	1.159	0.02110
Other non-health waiver	11,345	0.983	0.73900
Scheduled months in DEP	138,656	0.943	0.00000

Table 2.11—continued

Variable	Observations	Risk Ratio	p
Three-year enlistment	367,583	0.903	0.00000
Five-year enlistment	80,166	1.227	0.00000
Six-year enlistment	68,620	1.069	0.00460
AFQT categories 1–3A	520,088	0.906	0.00000
Physical capacity = 3	29,541	1.070	0.03150
Upper extremities = 3	5,240	0.814	0.01740
Lower extremities = 3	8,114	1.133	0.03930
Hearing = 3	5,522	1.042	0.60400
Vision = 3	10,055	1.062	0.27600
Psychiatric = 3	6,929	2.918	0.00000
BMI decile 1	72,308	1.154	0.00000
BMI decile 2	73,896	1.037	0.21000
BMI decile 3	74,347	1.017	0.55900
BMI decile 4	74,862	1.004	0.89900
BMI decile 6	75,990	1.014	0.64600
BMI decile 7	76,351	1.038	0.20900
BMI decile 8	76,793	1.030	0.32900
BMI decile 9	77,079	1.026	0.39500
BMI decile 10	75,361	1.115	0.00029
Passed TTAS 112 cutoff	21,344	0.682	0.00000
Took and passed ARMS	3,785	0.929	0.35900
Accession year FY02	74,017	1.958	0.00000
Accession year FY03	70,500	2.537	0.00000
Accession year FY04	77,449	3.096	0.00000
Accession year FY05	68,993	2.465	0.00000
Accession year FY06	78,247	2.464	0.00000

Table 2.11—continued

Variable	Observations	Risk Ratio	p
Accession year FY07	78,575	3.166	0.00000
Accession year FY08	79,070	3.953	0.00000
Accession year FY09	68,293	3.997	0.00000
Accession year FY10	73,841	3.320	0.00000
Accession year FY11	63,268	2.695	0.00000
Accession month January	89,715	0.985	0.62600
Accession month February	65,142	1.023	0.47500
Accession month March	61,568	1.028	0.39400
Accession month April	60,434	1.101	0.00318
Accession month June	80,268	0.983	0.60200
Accession month July	84,261	0.943	0.06400
Accession month August	85,980	0.997	0.92200
Accession month September	66,804	1.057	0.08140
Accession month October	71,435	1.052	0.10600
Accession month November	57,828	0.995	0.87400
Accession month December	13,069	1.013	0.83200
Prior service	76,013	0.418	0.00000

experience such an early separation than a female recruit, other things equal. There was little difference in the rate of such separations by recruits' years of age or their marital or children status. Minority recruits were 30–50 percent less likely to experience a separation for a physical condition other than a disability relative to white, non-Hispanic recruits. Recruits who had four-year college degrees were about one-third less likely to experience a such a separation, whereas recruits who held GED degrees were about 25 percent more likely to experience one than were recruits with traditional high school diplomas. Recruits with non-traffic offense waivers were about 15 percent less likely to experience a separation for a physical condition other than a disability than were recruits without waivers. The difference across scheduled months in the DEP was limited. Recruits enlisting for five-year terms of service were about 20–25 percent more likely to experience a separation for a physical condition other than a disability than four-year enlistees. The reason for this difference is not clear; it could possibly be related to the occupational specialties for which five-year terms were common during the study period or, perhaps, to their longer exposure than those with four-year terms, given that recruits with three-year terms were nearly 10 percent less likely to experience this type of separation. Recruits with serious limitations indicated on the psychiatric PULHES measure were nearly three times as likely to experience a separation for a physical condition other than a disability than were recruits with fewer/no limitations on the psychiatric measure. Recruits who were well under average weight for their height (BMI decile 1) were about 15 percent more likely to experience a separation for a physical condition other than a disability than were recruits of average weight for their height (BMI decile 5). Recruits who scored 112 or better on the TTAS test were about one-third less likely to separate for a physical condition other than a disability than were recruits who scored lower. Relative to recruits who accessed in FY01, recruits accessing in later years were more likely to experience a separation for a physical condition other than a disability. There were no differences in the rates of such separations by month of accession. Last, recruits with prior military service were only about 40 percent as likely to experience a separation for a physical condition other than a disability as those without prior service, all else equal.

The results of our logistic regression analysis of experiencing a separation for failing a medical or physical standard are shown in Table 2.12. We found that a male recruit was about 60 percent as likely to experience such an early separation than was a female recruit, other things equal. In contrast, recruits over 30 years of age were about 35–45 percent more likely to experience a separation for a medical or physical condition than recruits of ages 17–21. Married recruits were about 10–15 percent more likely to experience such a separation than recruits who had never been married and had no children; formerly married recruits with children were about 30 percent more likely to

Table 2.12
Separation for Failing a Medical or Physical Standard (N = 795,940; separation rate for failing a medical or physical standard = 3.5 percent)

Variable	Observations	Risk Ratio	p
Male	663,365	0.591	0.00000
Age at contract 22–24	135,629	0.966	0.05260
Age at contract 25–30	103,799	1.093	0.00005
Age at contract 31–35	29,824	1.363	0.00000
Age at contract 36+	13,733	1.453	0.00000
Married, kids	98,481	1.136	0.00000
Married, no kids	57,760	1.117	0.00000
Formerly married, kids	8,551	1.301	0.00000
Formerly married, no kids	9,758	1.211	0.00026
Never married, kids	17,974	1.126	0.00256
Asian	25,318	0.460	0.00000
African-American	136,340	0.589	0.00000
Hispanic	84,668	0.526	0.00000
Other non-white non-Hispanic	12,955	0.584	0.00000
Some college	73,113	0.893	0.00000
Four-year college degree	37,339	0.516	0.00000
GED holder	114,107	1.343	0.00000
Traffic offense waiver	2,184	0.659	0.00024
Non-traffic offense waiver	49,507	0.873	0.00000
Drug/alcohol waiver	8,548	0.875	0.02540
Weight waiver	4,002	1.020	0.78700
Other health waiver	5,741	1.368	0.00000
Other non-health waiver	11,345	0.996	0.94300

Table 2.12—continued

Variable	Observations	Risk Ratio	p
Scheduled months in DEP	138,656	0.947	0.00000
Three-year enlistment	367,583	1.054	0.00031
Five-year enlistment	80,166	1.001	0.95600
Six-year enlistment	68,620	0.961	0.08810
AFQT categories 1–3A	520,088	0.830	0.00000
Physical capacity = 3	29,541	1.809	0.00000
Upper extremities = 3	5,240	2.289	0.00000
Lower extremities = 3	8,114	2.961	0.00000
Hearing = 3	5,522	1.229	0.00174
Vision = 3	10,055	1.217	0.00008
Psychiatric = 3	6,929	1.318	0.00000
BMI decile 1	72,308	1.135	0.00000
BMI decile 2	73,896	1.028	0.33400
BMI decile 3	74,347	0.991	0.75000
BMI decile 4	74,862	0.961	0.16600
BMI decile 6	75,990	1.014	0.62700
BMI decile 7	76,351	1.068	0.02130
BMI decile 8	76,793	1.162	0.00000
BMI decile 9	77,079	1.209	0.00000
BMI decile 10	75,361	1.471	0.00000
Passed TTAS 112 cutoff	21,344	0.699	0.00000
Took and passed ARMS	3,785	0.883	0.15300
Accession year FY02	74,017	5.834	0.00000
Accession year FY03	70,500	6.596	0.00000
Accession year FY04	77,449	6.819	0.00000

Table 2.12—continued

Variable	Observations	Risk Ratio	p
Accession year FY05	68,993	5.918	0.00000
Accession year FY06	78,247	2.953	0.00000
Accession year FY07	78,575	3.423	0.00000
Accession year FY08	79,070	4.064	0.00000
Accession year FY09	68,293	4.334	0.00000
Accession year FY10	73,841	3.607	0.00000
Accession year FY11	63,268	3.827	0.00000
Accession month January	89,715	1.012	0.66700
Accession month February	65,142	0.987	0.63400
Accession month March	61,568	1.005	0.87200
Accession month April	60,434	0.923	0.00795
Accession month June	80,268	0.924	0.00818
Accession month July	84,261	0.865	0.00000
Accession month August	85,980	0.899	0.00020
Accession month September	66,804	0.973	0.34700
Accession month October	71,435	0.962	0.18400
Accession month November	57,828	1.030	0.31900
Accession month December	13,069	0.988	0.83500
Prior service	76,013	0.082	0.00000

separate for this reason. Minority recruits were 40–55 percent less likely to experience a separation for failing a medical or physical standard relative to white, non-Hispanic recruits. Recruits with some college were about 10 percent less likely to experience a separation for failing a medical or physical standard, and those who had four-year college degrees were about half as likely to experience one, whereas recruits who held GED degrees were about one-third more likely to experience one than were recruits with traditional high school diplomas. Recruits with non-traffic offense waivers were 10–15 percent less likely to experience a separation for failing a medical or physical standard than recruits without waivers, whereas those with waivers for a prior health condition not involving serious limitations indicated on a PULHES measure were 35 percent more likely to experience one. The difference across scheduled time in the DEP was limited. Term of service also was not strongly associated with separation for failing a medical or physical standard. In contrast, recruits in AFQT categories 1–3A were about 15–20 percent less likely to experience such a separation than recruits with lower aptitude. Separation for failing a medical or physical standard was about two to three times as likely for recruits with serious limitations indicated on the physical capacity, upper extremities, or lower extremities PULHES measures than for recruits with fewer/no limitations on these measures. Recruits with serious psychiatric limitations were 30 percent more likely to experience a separation for failing a medical or physical standard than recruits with fewer/no limitations on this measure. Recruits who were well below average weight for their height (BMI decile = 1) were 10–15 percent more likely to experience a separation for failing a medical or physical standard than recruits of average weight for their height (BMI decile = 5), as also were those in BMI decile 8. Recruits in BMI decile 9 were 20 percent more likely to do so, and those well above average weight for their height (BMI decile 10) were nearly 50 percent more likely to experience a separation for failing a medical or physical standard than were recruits of average weight for their height (BMI decile 5). Recruits who scored 112 or better on the TTAS test were about 30 percent less likely to separate for failing a medical or physical standard than recruits who scored lower. Relative to recruits who accessed in FY01, recruits accessing in later years were more likely to experience a separation for failing a medical or physical standard. There were limited differences in the rates of separation for failing a medical or physical standard by month of accession; the rate for July recruits, disproportionately graduating high school seniors, was about 15 percent lower than for May accessions. Last, recruits with prior military service were only about 10 percent as likely to experience a separation for failing to meet a medical or physical standard as those without prior service, all else equal.

The results of our logistic regression analysis of experiencing a separation for a serious offense are shown in Table 2.13. We found that a male recruit was more than twice as likely to experience such a separation than a female recruit, other things equal. In contrast, older recruits were about one-third to two-thirds less likely to experience such a separation than recruits of ages 17–21, the odds decreasing with age. Married recruits were about 20–25 percent less likely to experience a separation for a serious offense than recruits who had never been married and had no children. The results for minority recruits varied: Asian recruits were 40 percent less likely to experience a separation for a serious offense relative to white, non-Hispanic recruits; in contrast, African-American recruits were 50 percent more likely to experience one. Recruits with some college were about 25 percent less likely to experience a separation for a serious offense, and those who had four-year college degrees were about 60 percent less likely to experience one; in contrast, recruits who held GED degrees were almost 60 percent more likely to experience a separation for a serious offense than were recruits with traditional high school diplomas. Recruits with offense or drug/alcohol waivers were much more likely than recruits without waivers to be separated due to a serious offense; the separation rates increased by about two-thirds for the offense waivers (the traffic offense waiver result falls short of the $p < .00001$ criterion) to more than twice the rate for recruits with drug/alcohol waivers. The difference across scheduled time in the DEP was very large, with the likelihood of a separation for a serious offense decreasing with more time spent in the DEP, perhaps due to attrition among recruits experiencing early problems. Recruits with longer terms of service had a greater likelihood of separating for a serious offense: Those with three-year terms were about 25 percent less likely to do so than recruits with four-year terms; those with five-year terms were similar to those with four-year terms; while recruits with six-year terms were about 30 percent more likely separate for a serious offense. Recruits in AFQT categories 1–3A were about 15–20 percent less likely to experience such a separation than recruits with lower aptitude. Separation for a serious offense was not

Table 2.13
Separation for a Serious Offense (N = 795,940; separation rate for a serious offense = 2.0 percent)

Variable	Observations	Risk Ratio	p
Male	663,365	2.242	0.00000
Age at contract 22–24	135,629	0.685	0.00000
Age at contract 25–30	103,799	0.539	0.00000
Age at contract 31–35	29,824	0.469	0.00000
Age at contract 36+	13,733	0.306	0.00000
Married, kids	98,481	0.808	0.00000
Married, no kids	57,760	0.770	0.00000
Formerly married, kids	8,551	1.140	0.15900
Formerly married, no kids	9,758	1.183	0.05140
Never married, kids	17,974	1.124	0.01560
Asian	25,318	0.590	0.00000
African-American	136,340	1.567	0.00000
Hispanic	84,668	0.982	0.51700
Other non-white non-Hispanic	12,955	1.271	0.00006
Some college	73,113	0.757	0.00000
Four-year college degree	37,339	0.377	0.00000
GED holder	114,107	1.571	0.00000
Traffic offense waiver	2,184	1.751	0.00016
Non-traffic offense waiver	49,507	1.647	0.00000
Drug/alcohol waiver	8,548	2.281	0.00000
Weight waiver	4,002	0.996	0.97700
Other health waiver	5,741	0.879	0.15600
Other non-health waiver	11,345	1.035	0.69100
Scheduled months in DEP	138,656	0.862	0.00000

Table 2.13—continued

Variable	Observations	Risk Ratio	p
Three-year enlistment	367,583	0.741	0.00000
Five-year enlistment	80,166	1.088	0.00257
Six-year enlistment	68,620	1.297	0.00000
AFQT categories 1–3A	520,088	0.822	0.00000
Physical capacity = 3	29,541	0.827	0.00010
Upper extremities = 3	5,240	0.814	0.06740
Lower extremities = 3	8,114	0.876	0.14500
Hearing = 3	5,522	1.182	0.07950
Vision = 3	10,055	0.799	0.00969
Psychiatric = 3	6,929	1.258	0.00279
BMI decile 1	72,308	0.989	0.75800
BMI decile 2	73,896	0.998	0.95000
BMI decile 3	74,347	1.028	0.41400
BMI decile 4	74,862	0.997	0.93100
BMI decile 6	75,990	0.925	0.03140
BMI decile 7	76,351	0.905	0.00616
BMI decile 8	76,793	0.862	0.00006
BMI decile 9	77,079	0.854	0.00002
BMI decile 10	75,361	0.792	0.00000
Passed TTAS 112 cutoff	21,344	1.086	0.04120
Took and passed ARMS	3,785	0.924	0.54200
Accession year FY02	74,017	0.874	0.00101
Accession year FY03	70,500	0.773	0.00000
Accession year FY04	77,449	0.883	0.00250
Accession year FY05	68,993	0.816	0.00000
Accession year FY06	78,247	0.956	0.24600

Table 2.13—continued

Variable	Observations	Risk Ratio	p
Accession year FY07	78,575	1.096	0.01700
Accession year FY08	79,070	1.264	0.00000
Accession year FY09	68,293	1.523	0.00000
Accession year FY10	73,841	1.728	0.00000
Accession year FY11	63,268	1.520	0.00000
Accession month January	89,715	0.907	0.00686
Accession month February	65,142	0.824	0.00000
Accession month March	61,568	0.912	0.01980
Accession month April	60,434	0.948	0.17700
Accession month June	80,268	0.946	0.14900
Accession month July	84,261	0.961	0.28300
Accession month August	85,980	0.918	0.01990
Accession month September	66,804	0.874	0.00072
Accession month October	71,435	0.879	0.00086
Accession month November	57,828	0.870	0.00058
Accession month December	13,069	0.922	0.24900
Prior service	76,013	0.975	0.52400

significantly associated at $p < .00001$ with serious limitations indicated on the PULHES measures. In contrast, recruits who were above average weight for their height (BMI deciles 8–10) were about 15–20 percent less likely to experience a separation for a serious offense as those in BMI decile 5; the differences for BMI deciles 8 and 9 approached but did not quite reach $p < .00001$. Relative to recruits who accessed in FY01, recruits accessing in FY03 and FY05 were about 20 percent less likely to have separated for a serious offense, whereas recruits accessing in FY08–FY11 were 25–75 percent more likely to have done so. There were limited differences in the rates of separation for a serious offense by month of accession; the rate for February recruits was about 15–20 percent lower than for May accessions.

The results of our logistic regression analysis of experiencing a separation for drug abuse are shown in Table 2.14. We found that a male recruit was more than twice as likely to experience such an early separation than was a female recruit, other things equal. In contrast, recruits over 21 years of age were about 15–50 percent less likely to experience a separation for drug abuse than were recruits ages 17–21; the likelihood decreased with age at accession. Married recruits were about 30 percent less likely to experience such a separation than recruits who had never been married and had no children. Asian recruits were about one-third less likely to experience a separation for drug abuse relative to white, non-Hispanic recruits; African-American recruits were about two-thirds more likely to experience one. Recruits with some college were about one-third less likely to experience a separation for drug abuse, and those who had four-year college degrees were only about 25 percent as likely to experience one. In contrast, recruits who held GED degrees were about 40 percent more likely to experience a separation for drug abuse than were recruits with traditional high school diplomas. Recruits with traffic or non-traffic offense waivers were twice less likely to experience a separation for drug abuse than were recruits without waivers, and those with drug/alcohol waivers were four times as likely to experience one. The difference across scheduled time in the DEP was substantial, with the likelihood of a separation for drug abuse decreasing with more time spent in the DEP, perhaps due to attrition among recruits experiencing early problems. Recruits with three-year terms of service were about 25 percent less likely to experience a separation for drug abuse than recruits with four-year terms, perhaps due to the smaller period of exposure. Recruits who were above average weight for their height (BMI deciles 7–10) were about 15–30 percent less likely to experience a separation for drug abuse as those in BMI decile 5; the difference increased with BMI. Since there is only one reason for separation coded, the difference could be related to the greater rates of entry-level performance and physical standard separations for recruits with high BMI ratios. Recruits who scored 112 or better on the TTAS test were about 15–20 percent more likely to separate for drug abuse

Table 2.14
Separation for Drug Abuse (N = 795,940; separation rate for drug abuse = 2.6 percent)

Variable	Observations	Risk Ratio	p
Male	663,365	2.298	0.00000
Age at contract 22–24	135,629	0.827	0.00000
Age at contract 25–30	103,799	0.733	0.00000
Age at contract 31–35	29,824	0.686	0.00000
Age at contract 36+	13,733	0.496	0.00000
Married, kids	98,481	0.697	0.00000
Married, no kids	57,760	0.709	0.00000
Formerly married, kids	8,551	1.072	0.37300
Formerly married, no kids	9,758	0.867	0.09990
Never married, kids	17,974	1.173	0.00005
Asian	25,318	0.640	0.00000
African-American	136,340	1.639	0.00000
Hispanic	84,668	0.948	0.03520
Other non-white non-Hispanic	12,955	0.935	0.27700
Some college	73,113	0.682	0.00000
Four-year college degree	37,339	0.228	0.00000
GED holder	114,107	1.412	0.00000
Traffic offense waiver	2,184	2.111	0.00000
Non-traffic offense waiver	49,507	2.043	0.00000
Drug/alcohol waiver	8,548	4.047	0.00000
Weight waiver	4,002	0.796	0.05740
Other health waiver	5,741	1.068	0.38500
Other non-health waiver	11,345	0.859	0.05940
Scheduled months in DEP	138,656	0.782	0.00000

Table 2.14—continued

Variable	Observations	Risk Ratio	p
Three-year enlistment	367,583	0.764	0.00000
Five-year enlistment	80,166	0.946	0.02850
Six-year enlistment	68,620	1.085	0.00096
AFQT categories 1–3A	520,088	0.941	0.00014
Physical capacity = 3	29,541	0.825	0.00001
Upper extremities = 3	5,240	1.020	0.82700
Lower extremities = 3	8,114	0.781	0.00365
Hearing = 3	5,522	0.985	0.87300
Vision = 3	10,055	0.790	0.00219
Psychiatric = 3	6,929	0.921	0.29200
BMI decile 1	72,308	1.108	0.00053
BMI decile 2	73,896	1.114	0.00022
BMI decile 3	74,347	1.059	0.05200
BMI decile 4	74,862	0.994	0.84400
BMI decile 6	75,990	0.917	0.00627
BMI decile 7	76,351	0.839	0.00000
BMI decile 8	76,793	0.768	0.00000
BMI decile 9	77,079	0.765	0.00000
BMI decile 10	75,361	0.717	0.00000
Passed TTAS 112 cutoff	21,344	1.168	0.00000
Took and passed ARMS	3,785	1.181	0.10800
Accession year FY02	74,017	1.027	0.48800
Accession year FY03	70,500	1.219	0.00000
Accession year FY04	77,449	1.312	0.00000
Accession year FY05	68,993	1.276	0.00000
Accession year FY06	78,247	1.283	0.00000

Table 2.14—continued

Variable	Observations	Risk Ratio	p
Accession year FY07	78,575	1.583	0.00000
Accession year FY08	79,070	1.697	0.00000
Accession year FY09	68,293	1.855	0.00000
Accession year FY10	73,841	2.173	0.00000
Accession year FY11	63,268	2.097	0.00000
Accession month January	89,715	0.950	0.11600
Accession month February	65,142	0.914	0.01000
Accession month March	61,568	1.014	0.69200
Accession month April	60,434	0.940	0.08100
Accession month June	80,268	1.008	0.81400
Accession month July	84,261	0.985	0.67300
Accession month August	85,980	1.031	0.34800
Accession month September	66,804	1.076	0.03180
Accession month October	71,435	0.981	0.56500
Accession month November	57,828	0.952	0.17000
Accession month December	13,069	0.909	0.14400
Prior service	76,013	0.685	0.00000

than were recruits who scored lower. Relative to recruits who accessed in FY01, recruits accessing in FY03–FY11 were more likely to have experienced a separation for drug abuse; the likelihood of a drug abuse separation increased in later years. There were limited differences in the rates of separation for drug abuse by month of accession. Last, recruits with prior military service were about one-third less likely to experience a separation for drug abuse than those without prior service, all else equal.

Table 2.15 summarizes our primary results for reasons for separation. As noted for Table 2.6, given the very large number of observations, here, for the primary effects, we focus only on differences of

Table 2.15
Summary of Separation Reason Results

Variable	Entry-Level Performance and Conduct	Physical Condition, Not a Disability	Failing a Medical or Physical Standard	Serious Offense	Drug Abuse
Male	–	–	–	+	+
Age at contract 22–24				–	
Age at contract 25–30				–	–
Age at contract 31–35			+	–	–
Age at contract 36+			+	–	–
Married, kids				–	–
Married, no kids				–	–
Formerly married, kids			+		
Formerly married, no kids					
Never married, kids					
Asian		–	–	–	–
African-American		–	–	+	+
Hispanic	–	–	–		
Other non-white non-Hispanic	–	–	–		
Some college				–	–
Four-year college degree	–	–	–	–	–
GED holder	+	+	+	+	+
Traffic offense waiver					+
Non-traffic offense waiver				+	+

Table 2.15—continued

Variable	Entry-Level Performance and Conduct	Physical Condition, Not a Disability	Failing a Medical or Physical Standard	Serious Offense	Drug Abuse
Drug/alcohol waiver				+	+
Weight waiver					
Other health waiver	+		+		
Other non-health waiver					
Scheduled months in DEP				–	–
Three-year enlistment				–	–
Five-year enlistment	–	+			
Six-year enlistment				+	
AFQT categories 1–3A	–				
Physical capacity = 3			+		
Upper extremities = 3	–		+		
Lower extremities = 3			+		
Hearing = 3					
Vision = 3					
Psychiatric = 3	+	+	+		
BMI decile 1					
BMI decile 2					
BMI decile 3					
BMI decile 4					
BMI decile 6					
BMI decile 7					

Table 2.15—continued

Variable	Entry-Level Performance and Conduct	Physical Condition, Not a Disability	Failing a Medical or Physical Standard	Serious Offense	Drug Abuse
BMI decile 8	+				–
BMI decile 9	+		+		–
BMI decile 10	+		+	–	–
Passed TTAS 112 cutoff	–	–	–		
Took and passed ARMS					
Prior service	–	–	–		–

20 percent or greater in the reason for separation and only when the probability of observing the difference by chance is less than one in 100,000. The plus or minus signs show the direction of the association with the reason for separation.

As discussed earlier, using the factors found to be the primary drivers of the outcomes in the regression results, all else equal, we built a tool to estimate the prospective effects on outcomes and costs of making single or multiple changes in recruit cohort characteristics. Unlike the regressions, the tool allows all of the natural covariation among recruit characteristics to affect the simulation of training performance, the level and timing of attrition, effects on adverse intermediate outcomes, and the rates and reasons for early separation. It also quantifies recruiting, training, and replacement costs associated with these alternative combinations. Possible differences in compensation costs associated with these changes also are considered when the number of recruits with prior military service is changed. The regression risk ratios discussed in this chapter thus are not used directly by the tool. However, they provide important information in thinking about for which characteristics to vary enlistment representation in order to achieve specific objectives or to increase supply while minimizing the potential adverse effects of such changes, and, in some cases, concerning which specific factors are most highly associated with adverse outcomes and, thus, might be identifiers for recruit remediation. Tables 2.6, 2.9, and 2.15 should be particularly useful for these purposes.

We note that an important motivation for building a tool that allows all of the natural covariation among recruit characteristics to affect the simulation of the outcomes of interest in this research is that regression models that fully interact our predictors of each outcome are not feasible due to the underlying rates of the predictors and related multicollinearity issues. In this regard, we also note that classification trees might be used in addition to the regression results to gain further insights into associations of the predictors with each of the outcomes. This additional information would not require additional assumptions, and could suggest higher-order interactions. A disadvantage would be the instability of such trees. This can be addressed by generating multiple trees and then averaging the results, though such averaging complicates interpretation. Another reported disadvantage concerns capturing additive structures, which can be captured well by regressions.

CHAPTER THREE

Construction of Recruit Characteristic Selection Tool and Simulation of Effects of Changes in Recruit Characteristics

As discussed earlier, importantly, regressions identify the independent associations of specific recruit characteristics with specific outcomes. Thus, the regression analyses play a key role in identifying the main factors driving associations between recruit cohort characteristics and these outcomes that should be considered when assessing the effects of possible changes in enlistment eligibility rates on outcomes of interest—such as the effect of increasing or decreasing the eligibility of recruits with GEDs on first-term attrition—and can provide guidance in selection of possible eligibility rate changes connected with the Army's overall goals.

In actuality, specific characteristics are not independent of one another. For example, age is related to marital or children status, education level is related to aptitude, and gender is related to the BMI, race/ethnicity, and term of service of recruits. Therefore, when used as screeners to help screen in or screen out potential recruits, specific factors do not act in isolation, as they do in a regression. Rather, changes in the percentage of recruits with a specific characteristic bring with them changes in the percentages of other characteristics that covary with the screener. For this reason, we built a recruit selection tool for the Army that includes the covariation among the key factors identified in our regression analyses in assessing the potential effects of eligibility rate changes for specific recruit characteristics on outcomes of interest.

The tool allows the user to make simultaneous changes in enlistment eligibility levels for multiple selection criteria.

Tool Database and Application

Overview

The tool database consists of the same recruit characteristics and outcomes used in the regression analyses and discussed in Chapter Two. It also includes recruiting and training costs for each recruit. These costs are described in detail below. The tool allows the user to choose the changes in recruit characteristics that he or she desires. In the example we discuss later in this chapter, we increase the percentage of Tier 2 recruits from 5 percent to 10 percent, increase the percentage of recruits with non-traffic offense waivers from 0 percent to 10 percent, and increase the number of recruits with prior military service from 3,000 to 5,000.[1] The outputs of simulating the changes in recruit characteristics cover changes in all of the outcomes assessed in the regression analyses, plus the related changes in training and recruiting costs. Recruiting costs are based on an annual estimate from Headquarters Department of the Army (Personnel) (HQDA G-1), which is constant across recruits. However, information from the Recruiting Resource Model (RRM) (Knapp et al., forthcoming) can be incorporated to consider changes in recruiting resource requirements per person due to the changes in recruit cohort characteristics, the size of the recruiting requirement, and the recruiting environment. The recruit selection tool includes a variety of training outcomes: Basic Combat Training (BCT), Advanced Individual Training (AIT), One Station Unit Training (OSUT), and IET (covering both basic and occupation training as whole).

The tool database is illustrated conceptually in Figure 3.1. It consists a vector of information (row) for each of the approximately

[1] As noted earlier, historically, Army practice has been to insist on greater AFQT category 1–3A levels among Tier 2 recruits. For this reason, as discussed later in this chapter, the percentage of AFQT category 1–3As also is adjusted when the percentage of Tier 2 recruits is adjusted.

Figure 3.1
Overview of Recruit Selection Tool Database

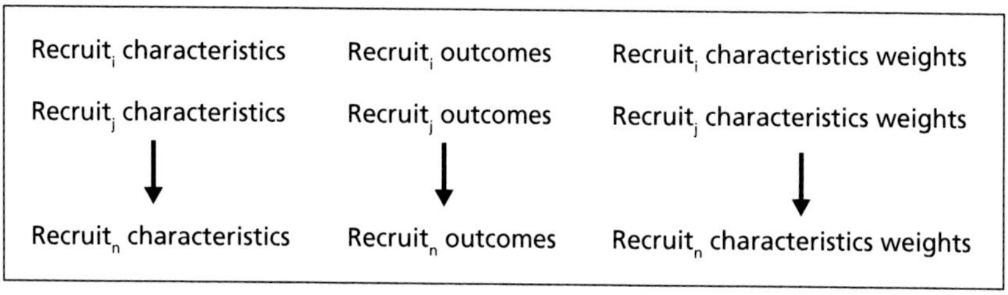

RAND *RR2267-3.1*

870,000 recruits into the Army during FY01–FY11. The information covers the recruit's values for each of the characteristics (and the left-out reference group for characteristics with more than two values, such as age at enlistment) included in the regressions discussed earlier in Chapter Two and summarized for convenience in Table 3.1. It also includes the values of the outcomes shown in Table 3.2 for the given recruit. The outcomes are discussed in greater detail below. Last, the information vector for the recruit also contains a weight for each of the recruit's characteristics. The weights all are initialized equal to a value of 1.0. The user chooses the desired levels of the recruit characteristics he or she wishes to change. New weights are derived by the tool for each value of each of the characteristics chosen by the user in order to produce the new targeted levels for these characteristics. The product of the weights in each row (recruit) in the database for the characteristics chosen by the user is applied to that recruit based on his or her values on these characteristics (for example, Tier 2 or not, non-traffic offense waiver or not, prior military service or not). The weighted results are then averaged over all rows (recruits) to determine the new aggregated outcome levels.

We note that the tool also can be used to investigate the prospective outcomes of changes in recruit eligibility within subgroups, for example:

- recruits with specific characteristics included in the tool

- recruits into specific occupational specialties (career management fields [CMFs]/military occupational specialities [MOSs])
- results for specific Occupational Physical Assessment Test (OPAT) categories (using the MOS crosswalk into OPAT categories).

Appendix C provides information on examining the prospective outcomes of changes in recruit eligibility within subgroups.

Recruit Characteristics

As noted, the tool database includes the same recruit characteristics and outcomes used in the regression analyses for each recruit into the active enlisted force during FY01–FY11. The characteristics are shown in Table 3.1.

Characteristics primarily consist of information about a recruit collected during the recruiting process. The exceptions are two characteristics of the enlistment contract: DEP length (months scheduled in the DEP) and length of term of service. For each recruit and characteristic, we give a value of one or zero depending on whether the recruit has the specific characteristic. For variables that can have more than two values, such as "Age at enlistment contract," we include all the binary variables used in the regression models plus the left-out group (ages 22–24, 25–30, 31–35, 36+, and 17–21). For binary variables, we only need to include the variable used in the models. Only number of months scheduled in the DEP is left as a continuous variable.

Outcomes

In the database, after the recruit characteristics come a series of outcomes for each recruit. Most all of the behavioral outcomes are also defined as binary variables, where a one indicates that someone attrited at a given point, or for a given reason in the case of the Separation Program Designator (SPD) codes, or that the soldier experienced a particular negative personnel action such as a reenlistment prohibition, and a zero indicates that he or she did not do so. The outcome variables in the database are shown in Table 3.2.

The variables include DEP attrition; training attrition codes broken out into detail based on which course(s) an enlistee took, BCT,

Table 3.1
Recruit Characteristics Included in Recruit Selection Tool

Recruit Characteristic
Gender (male vs. female)
Age at enlistment contract (22–24, 25–30, 31–35, 36+ vs. 17–21)
Marital and children status (married, kids; married, no kids; formerly married, kids; formerly married, no kids; single, kids vs. single, no kids)
Race/ethnicity (Asian, African-American, Hispanic, other non-white non-Hispanic vs. white non-Hispanic)
Attended college (some college, graduated college vs. no college)
Enlistment waiver (traffic offense; non-traffic offense; drug/alcohol waiver; weight waiver; other health prior condition waiver when no PULHES measure = 3; other non-offense, non-health waiver vs. no waiver)
Months scheduled to be in the DEP
First term length (2 [DEP attrition only], 3, 5, 6 vs. 4 years)
Education tier (Tier 2 vs. Tier 1)
AFQT category (1–3A vs. 3B–4)
PULHES-related significant limitations (3 vs. <3, for the physical capacity, upper extremities, lower extremities, hearing, vision, and psychiatric ratings)
BMI (each BMI decile vs. decile 5)
TTAS score (passed with 112 cutoff vs. did not pass)
ARMS score (passed vs. did not pass)
Prior military service (yes vs. no)
Contract/accession year (FY02–FY11 by year vs. FY01)
Contract/accession month (January–April, June–December by month vs. May)

AIT, or OSUT; attrition during term of enlistment; number of months actually served in term of enlistment; negative rank change (demotion); bar to reenlistment; suspension of favorable person status; and SPD codes. The SPD codes include:

- CR: Weight Control
- DB: Hardship

Table 3.2
Recruit Outcomes Included in Recruit Selection Tool

Behavioral Outcomes	Cost Outcomes
Average months served in first (contract) term	Average recruiting cost (USD, thousands)
% attrited during first term	Average training cost, full (USD, thousands)
% bar to reenlistment	Average training cost, half (USD, thousands)
% suspension of favorable person status	Average total cost, full (USD, thousands)
% negative rank change	Average total cost, half (USD, thousands)
% SPD: Weight control failure	Total accession cost (USD, millions)
% SPD: Hardship	Total training cost, full (USD, millions)
% SPD: Pregnancy or childbirth	Total training cost, half (USD, millions)
% SPD: Parenthood/custody minor children	Total cost, full (USD, millions)
% SPD: in lieu of trial by court-martial	Total cost, half (USD, millions)
% SPD: Physical standards	Change in total accession cost (USD, millions)
% SPD: Condition, not a disability	Change in total training cost, full (USD, millions)
% SPD: Fail medical/physical standard	Change in total training cost, half (USD, millions)
% SPD: Personality disorder	Change in total cost, full (USD, millions)
% SPD: Entry level performance and conduct	Change in total cost, half (USD, millions)
% SPD: Unsatisfactory performance	
% SPD: Court martial conviction—other	
% SPD: Pattern of misconduct	
% SPD: Misconduct, absent without leave	
% SPD: Misconduct, drug abuse	
% SPD: Commission of a serious offense	
% SPD: Desertion	
% SPD: Failed entry	
% SPD: Other misconduct	
% SPD: Failed rehab	
% failed AIT	
% failed BCT	
% failed IET	
% failed OSUT	

- DF: Pregnancy or Childbirth
- DG: Parenthood/Custody of Minor Children
- DZ: Desertion
- EZ: Failed Entry
- FS: In Lieu of Trial by Court-Martial
- FT: Physical Standard
- FV: Condition—Not a Disability
- FW: Fail Medical/Physical Standard
- FX: Personality Disorder
- GA: Entry-Level Performance and Conduct
- HJ: Unsatisfactory Performance
- JD: Court-Martial Conviction—Other
- KA: Pattern of Misconduct
- KD: Misconduct—Absent Without Leave
- KK: Misconduct—Drug Abuse
- KQ: Commission of a Serious Offense
- KZ: Other Misconduct
- PZ: Failed Rehab.

The training outcomes include:

- Failed AIT on first attempt—no other attempts taken
- Failed AIT on multiple attempts—never passed
- Failed BCT on first attempt—no other attempts taken
- Failed BCT on multiple attempts—never passed
- Failed IET on first attempt—no other attempts taken
- Failed IET on multiple attempts—never passed
- Failed OSUT on first attempt—no other attempts taken
- Failed OSUT on multiple attempts—never passed.

The outcome information included for each recruit covers the period FY01–FY16 (first three quarters) while the recruit was in the enlistment term of service.

Recruiting costs are based on an annual estimate from HQDA G-1, which is constant across recruits. However, information from the RRM (Knapp et al., forthcoming) can be incorporated to consider changes in recruiting resource requirements per person due to the changes in recruit cohort characteristics (involving recruit quality, enlistment waivers, or prior service), the recruiting environment, and the recruiting goals (including things such as the numbers of accessions and contracts needed). Training costs per recruit are based on the full cost of a course for those completing it or, alternatively for recruits failing the course, full or half cost, depending on the outcome measure (both measures are calculated by the tool).

Derivation of IET-Related Training Cost Metrics

In this section, we describe the methodology for the calculation of training costs. The contribution of the methodology is differentiating training costs among those that passed and those that failed, and among those that were given more than one "try" in attaining a training goal before their final disposition was determined.

Definition of a Training "Try"

To complete IET, enlisted soldiers must pass BCT and AIT or, for certain MOSs, OSUT. Some trainees make more than one attempt at training in those three areas (BCT, AIT, or OSUT) before a final resolution is reached. A "try" is defined as an enrollment in a specific Army Training Requirements and Resources System (ATRRS) class. In this analysis, we are interested in the number of times an individual enrolls in an IET-related training class (BCT, AIT, and OSUT) and in the final outcome in each instance.

All three types of courses most often end with a single class, either with a graduation or, much less frequently, with a failure. However, the final outcome is not always settled the first time a student enters a training class. There are also intermediate outcomes possible that may delay training or change training goals, and which require a student to enter more than one training class before a final resolution is determined.

The ATRRS OSTAT (output status) variable allows for six possible resolutions of a training enrollment (listed below). Besides graduation (the most common outcome), two outcomes represent a failure in the course, and the other three outcomes represent a delay in training or a change in training goals (i.e., change in MOS being trained) midway through the training process. In these cases, the trainee normally enrolls in a follow-up class to continue his or her training. The output status categories are as follows:

- G: Graduate, successfully completed class
- D: Discharged from the service
- Z: Other nonsuccessful completion
- L: Recycle out, to another class, same course
- K: Retrainee out, to another course of instruction
- H: Hold (showed did not start or did not graduate).

Individual-Level Training Outcomes for IET Based on the Number of Tries

Using training tries as an intermediate outcome, we defined four final outcomes (see list below) for individuals in each of three types of training: BCT, AIT, and OSUT. We also derived these outcomes for IET as a whole, depending on outcomes in the other course-type categories. A single try for IET was either one BCT enrollment followed by (assuming BCT was passed) one AIT enrollment, or one OSUT enrollment. The four outcomes are

1. Passed on a single try
2. Passed on multiple tries
3. Failed on a single try
4. Failed on multiple tries.

We found that 2–12 percent of accessions required more than one try, depending on the type of training and whether the accession entered as a prior-service or non-prior-service recruit.[2] in addition, we found that most prior-service recruits did not need to repeat BCT and that a little over half of the prior-service recruits required no training

[2] More precisely, the percentages for passing on one try, passing after more than one try, failing on one try, and failing after more than one try were as follows: 90.5, 2.1, 6.9, and 0.5 percent for BCT; 84.4, 9.0, 4.0, and 2.6 percent for AIT; 85.2, 3.7, 10.2, and 0.9 percent for OSUT; and 79.6, 8.1, 10.1, and 2.2 percent for IET, respectively.

at all because they entered the Army in an MOS for which they were already qualified.

Establishing Average Cost per Graduate for Three Types of IET Training

The most basic inputs for training cost come from the Office of the Deputy Chief of Staff, G-1 (which, in turn, obtained the data from U.S. Army Training and Doctrine Command). It listed the following basic costs per graduate for the three types of IET courses as of December 2015:

BCT	$18,030
AIT	$29,200
OSUT	$29,300.

BCT and OSUT amounts include the cost of the reception battalion.

Calculation of Total IET Training Costs for Individuals

The total training cost for an individual was the sum of the costs of all the valid tries in that individual's record. When the outcome was a graduation, the full cost of a graduate was applied. However, for enrollments associated with any other output status (e.g., a failure, a recycle, or a switch to a new MOS), depending on the outcome measure, either the full cost or only half the total course cost of a graduate was applied (because the course likely was not completed). For example, for the preferred, half-cost outcome measure, if an individual passed BCT on the first try, but needed two tries to get through AIT (because he or she changed MOS or had to be recycled out of a class into another one for the same MOS), the total cost of that individual's training would be defined as follows:

$$\text{full BCT cost} + \text{half AIT cost} + \text{full AIT cost},$$

or

$$18{,}030 + 0.5 \times 29{,}200 + 29{,}200 = \$61{,}830.$$

Weights

The tool database also includes a set of characteristic weights for each recruit into the Army during FY01–FY11, as noted previously and illustrated in Figure 3.1. As noted, the weights all are initialized equal to a value of 1.0. The user chooses the desired levels of the recruit characteristics he or she wishes to change. New weights are derived by the tool for each characteristic chosen by the user to produce the new targeted level for the characteristics.

To move a characteristic from an average of X percent in the microdata (historical level) to Y percent (user-specified level), the weight used equals the ratio Y/X. Implicit in the calculation is that, as the characteristic (e.g., Tier 2) is weighted by Y/X, the recruits without that characteristic (in this example, Tier 1) are also adjusted, by (1 – Y)/(1 – X). In this example, suppose that the historical level for Tier 2 is 5 percent and that the user wants to consider an excursion that increases it to 10 percent. Each of the Tier 2 recruits (the "GED holder" recruits) is given a weight of 10/5 for the education tier weight. Tier 1 recruits are given a weight of 90/95 for the tier weight. If the user is interested in weighting one subgroup of a characteristic with more than two subgroups (e.g., race/ethnicity), this weighting procedure also results in scaling the other subgroups, such that the sum across the subgroups remains at 100 percent.

Simultaneous changes in the rates of multiple characteristics bring into play the underlying correlations among them in the weighting procedure. This means that the order in which the weights are calculated matters. For instance, building on the example for education tier just discussed, suppose that the user also wants to increase the waiver rate for non-traffic offenses from 5 percent to 10 percent. If there were no association between these two variables, each of the non-traffic offense waiver recruits would be given a weight of 10/5 for the non-traffic offense weight, as above for Tier 2. Recruits without this waiver would be given a weight of 90/95 for the non-traffic offense weight. Now, alternatively, suppose that there is an association between education tier and waivers for non-traffic offenses. Such an association could, for example, be generated by the Army being more selective with respect to its preferred education level for recruits it issues waivers to.

In such a case, the non-traffic offense waiver rate for Tier 2s might only be 2 percent instead of 5 percent. This implies that the overall non-traffic offense waiver rate for a 10 percent Tier 2 recruit cohort would be approximately 4.842 percent rather than 5.0 percent. To bring the non-traffic offense waiver rate to the user's target of 10 percent, the tool would adjust the weight applied to recruits with this waiver to 10/4.842; the non-traffic offense waiver weight applied to recruits without this waiver would be 90/95.158.

As discussed earlier, the tool optimizes the weighting sequence for these characteristics by using an iterative procedure that generates the weights for each possible sequence, calculates the sum of the absolute values of the differences of the final percentages for the characteristics from the target percentage values, and then chooses the sequence with the smallest sum of the absolute values in order to produce the new distribution of recruit characteristics closest to the values chosen by the user. The product of the weights for each recruit (row) in the database—using the weight values the tool calculates as described above for the characteristics for which the user is changing representation levels and the values of those characteristics for the particular recruit—is applied to the recruit. The weighted results are then averaged over all recruits (rows) to determine the new behavioral outcome and average cost outcome levels. The tool also provides the new, post-weighting distribution of the full set of recruit characteristics. There are additional steps in generating the total cost outcomes; they are described later in this chapter.

Illustration of Tool Application

In this section, we illustrate the application of the recruit selection tool to expand supply in challenging recruiting conditions such as those now faced by the Army. We simultaneously vary the representation of four different characteristics in the accession cohort.[3] They are the

[3] Although we do not vary it in the supply expansion application, the percentage of Hispanic recruits is set to 17 percent to reflect recent, greater representation of Hispanics relative to its historical level.

percentage of (1) Tier 2 (GED) recruits, (2) recruits with enlistment waivers,[4] (3) recruits with prior military service, and (4) AFQT category 1–3A recruits. These characteristics represent the ones the Army has relied on in the past to increase enlistment supply during difficult recruiting periods.[5] In the example below, we use the RRM to refine the recruiting cost estimates.[6] In the example, we start from an 80,000 accession requirement (a challenging past and possible future growth target we wish to illustrate) and assume an unemployment rate of 4.8 percent; the unemployment rate is based on an estimated rate for the FY18–FY19 time frame assuming the current unemployment rate gradually returns to a more average rate over the next several years.

Step 1: Set Baseline for Excursion

We now walk through the example scenario. Recent enlistment data or other user-specified baseline levels are used to calculate the weights

---

4 To be roughly consistent with past Army practice, we vary the percentage of legal offense waivers other than those involving traffic offenses from 0 percent to 10 percent, bringing the range of the total waiver rate from 10 percent to 20 percent.

5 Historically, there has been an inherent relationship between the percentage of Tier 2 recruits and the percentage of AFQT category 1–3A recruits. There are two reasons for this relationship, with offsetting effects. First, Army practice has been to recruit mostly AFQT category 1–3As among its Tier 2 recruits; the average over our database period was 80 percent 1–3A for Tier 2 recruits. Second, the Army also has generally lowered (increased) the percentage of AFQT category 1–3A recruits among Tier 1s at the times it has increased (decreased) Tier 2 recruits, though by a smaller amount, as part of adjusting supply and managing costs. This coincident change works in the opposite direction. Recruits who have a Tier 1 education credential and score in AFQT categories 1–3A are referred to as "high-quality" recruits, and they are a recruiting priority for the Army. In the excursion discussed in this chapter, we reduce the targeted percentage of high-quality recruits from 57 percent to 54 percent, roughly paralleling a change from the recent level in the Army to the floor it would consider to expand supply. This is accomplished by setting the percentage of Tier 2 recruits to 10 percent, the Office of the Secretary of Defense ceiling. At the rate of 80 percent AFQT category 1–3A for the Tier 2 recruits, this translates to an overall level of 62 percent AFQT category 1–3As. This compares to an AFQT category 1–3A level of 61 percent for the baseline high-quality recruit level of 57 percent.

6 The RRM accounts for the effects of changes in recruiting rates for high-quality, waivered, and prior service-recruits on recruiting costs, subject to the number of enlistment contracts needed and economic conditions. It does not directly account for changes in the percentages of other recruit characteristics.

needed to get the FY01–FY11 database to have the desired baseline characteristic levels for the excursion of interest. The tool first calculates the historical average of each variable we wish to adjust based on the FY01–FY11 enlistment data. In this example, we choose to set baseline Tier 2 recruits to 5 percent; set the percentage of non-traffic offense waivers to 0 percent (.001 percent, for computational reasons), which corresponds to an overall waiver rate of about 10 percent based on past Army practice; set the number of prior-service recruits to 3,000 (rounds to 3.7 percent); and set the baseline percentage of Hispanic recruits to its larger, recent value of 17 percent. The tool iteratively calculates the appropriate weights to provide the closest match to the targeted levels. Table 3.3 shows the historical values and the target baseline values for this scenario.

As previously stated, each of these variables can have some correlation with one another. When the tool iterates through every permutation of the five variables, it finds that the weight estimation order that mostly closely produces the desired baseline percentages is as follows: by prior service, followed by Tier 2, followed by race/ethnicity Hispanic, followed by non-traffic offense waiver, followed by AFQT category 1–3A. This order produces the values in the "Calculated Baseline" column of Table 3.4.

Table 3.3
Historical and Target Baseline Characteristic Levels for Example Scenario

Input	Historical	Target Baseline
Race/ethnicity: Hispanic	10.655%	17.0%
Non-traffic offense waiver	6.272%	0.0%
Tier 2	14.183%	5.0%
Prior service	9.438%	3.7%
AFQT category 1–3A	65.684%	61.0%

NOTE: For prior service, we calculate 3,000/80,000 and round to one decimal place, leading to 3.7 percent.

Table 3.4
Tool-Calculated Baseline Characteristic Levels for Example Scenario

Input	Historical	Target Baseline	Calculated Baseline
Race/ethnicity: Hispanic	10.655%	17.0%	17.341%
Non-traffic offense waiver	6.272%	0.0%	0.001%
Tier 2	14.183%	5.0%	4.961%
Prior service	9.438%	3.7%	3.707%
AFQT category 1–3A	65.684%	61.0%	61.000%

Step 2: Set Excursion Characteristic Levels

The weights for the desired recruit characteristic levels in the excursion being assessed are set in a similar fashion. The user-specified excursion levels are used to calculate the weights needed to move from the historical characteristic levels to the excursion levels. In this example, we choose to set excursion Tier 2 recruits to 10 percent, set the percentage of non-traffic offense waivers to 10 percent, set the number of prior-service recruits to 5,000 (6.3 percent), and set the excursion percentage of AFQT category 1–3A recruits to 62 percent. The combination of the changes in Tier 2 and AFQT category 1–3A recruits brings the percentage of high-quality recruits from 57 percent to 54 percent, as discussed previously. Table 3.5 shows the tool-calculated baseline and excursion values for this scenario produced by the optimal weighting sequence.

Step 3: Run Excursion

Using the tool-derived weights for the four-characteristic simultaneous adjustment example scenario produces the outcome measure results in Table 3.6. As shown in the table, first-term attrition is estimated at 33.781 percent for the baseline, but increases slightly to 33.849 percent under the example scenario.[7] Analogously, average months served in the contract term decreases from 36.291 to 35.950. The percentage of

---

[7] Our measure excludes the small percentage of two-year enlistees and credits completion of term at four years of service for recruits with terms of four to six years.

Table 3.5
Calculated Baseline and Excursion Characteristic Levels for Example Scenario

Input	Calculated Baseline	Target Excursion	Calculated Excursion
Race/ethnicity: Hispanic	17.341%	17.0%	17.000%
Non-traffic offense waiver	0.001%	10.0%	10.020%
Tier 2	4.961%	10.0%	9.911%
Prior service	3.707%	6.3%	6.300%
AFQT category 1–3A	61.000%	62.0%	62.011%

NOTE: For prior service, we calculate 5,000/80,000 and round to one decimal place, leading to 6.3%.

recruits who will experience a bar to reenlistment during their contact term is estimated to decrease slightly, from 29.267 percent to 29.203 percent. In contrast, the percentages of recruits with a demotion or suspension of favorable person status are estimated to increase by about one percentage point. By analogy, the estimated changes in the other outcome measures can be observed by comparing the first and second columns of percentages.[8] The bottom of Table 3.6 shows the

[8] The tool also produces an adjustment estimate for each outcome. The adjustment is conceptually related to the fact that the characteristics of recruits vary from year to year. Thus, when a user chooses to use the tool to examine a change in recruit characteristics, the distribution of recruits' accession years also is changed (or contract years for DEP loss analyses). The adjustment identifies potential differences in the estimates of the outcome levels related simply to changes in the distribution of recruits across the accession years in the database induced by the weighting of recruit characteristics rather than to those associated with the changes in recruit characteristics themselves. Our examination shows that the adjustments are almost always negligible. For example, for the outcomes in Table 3.6, the mean adjustment is –0.032 percent, and the median adjustment is –0.002 percent; the analogous results for the absolute value of the adjustment are 0.048 percent and 0.012 percent, respectively. For this reason, we ignore the adjustments in the estimates shown in the table and in those provided in this chapter.

The adjustment consists of taking the difference between two sum products involving the estimated effects of the year dummy coefficients from the logistic regression model predicting a given outcome variable. Two cases of weighted calculations are used: In one case, the tool uses the distribution of years resulting from the baseline characteristic weights; in

Table 3.6
Behavioral and Average Cost Outcome Levels for Example Scenario

Outcome	Calculated Baseline	Calculated Excursion
Average months served in first (contract) term	36.291	35.950
% Attrited during first term	33.781	33.849
% Bar to reenlistment	29.267	29.203
% Suspension of favorable person status	47.211	48.173
% Negative rank change	13.382	14.382
% SPD: Weight control failure	0.694	0.644
% SPD: Hardship	0.293	0.297
% SPD: Pregnancy or childbirth	1.629	1.474
% SPD: Parenthood/custody minor children	1.133	1.118
% SPD: In lieu of trial by court-martial	1.685	1.888
% SPD: Physical standards	0.539	0.482
% SPD: Condition, not a disability	3.053	3.004
% SPD: Fail medical/physical standard	3.505	3.448
% SPD: Personality disorder	0.655	0.669
% SPD: Entry level performance and conduct	3.586	3.390
% SPD: Unsatisfactory performance	0.808	0.755
% SPD: Court martial conviction—other	0.196	0.216
% SPD: Pattern of misconduct	1.693	1.820
% SPD: Misconduct, absent without leave	0.201	0.223
% SPD: Misconduct, drug abuse	2.337	2.658
% SPD: Commission of a serious offense	1.851	2.007
% SPD: Desertion	0.105	0.116
% SPD: Failed entry	0.228	0.227
% SPD: Other misconduct	0.241	0.256
% SPD: Failed rehab	0.267	0.312

Table 3.6—continued

Outcome	Calculated Baseline	Calculated Excursion
% Failed AIT	6.597	6.646
% Failed BCT	7.423	7.338
% Failed IET	12.345	12.231
% Failed OSUT	11.073	11.072
Average G-1 recruiting cost (unit: 1,000 USD)	26.067	26.067
Average training cost, full (unit: 1,000 USD)	44.266	43.334
Average training cost, half (unit: 1,000 USD)	41.036	40.181
Average total cost, full (unit: 1,000 USD)	70.333	69.401
Average total cost, half (unit: 1,000 USD)	67.103	66.248

estimated recruiting and training costs per recruit. As discussed earlier, the recruiting cost is taken directly from G-1's figure for FY15. As also discussed, the training cost information provided by G-1 also is used as an input. It is adjusted for each recruit to account for the types of courses and the number of courses of each type the recruit took before eventually passing or failing training. Either the full cost or half of the full cost for courses the recruit did not pass is applied, depending on the training cost measure.

Step 4: Calculation of Total Cost

The last thing to do after calculating the distributions of the inputs and outputs is to calculate a total cost for the scenario. This calculation requires adjusting for changes in average months served, because such changes require adjusting the accession goal in order to maintain first-term strength. The adjustment uses the number of months served

the second case, it uses the distribution of years resulting from the excursion characteristic weights. As discussed above, we found the adjustment factors to be very small. Still, in theory, an exception might be if the user wished to heavily weight a characteristic that was only observed in a very limited range of FYs, such as passed TTAS or ARMS. However, even in cases that involve TTAS and ARMS, we found that only extremely large increases in the representation of these recruits made the adjustment matter in practical terms.

on average in the baseline case and divides that by the average months served in the contract period calculated for the excursion. This ratio is then multiplied by the baseline accession goal. In this case the adjustment would be 36.291/35.950 × 80,000 = 80,759 accessions.[9]

The revised accession goal is multiplied by the average cost of training an individual in the excursion—in this excursion, the cost measure using half cost for incomplete courses is used. This procedure generates an estimated value of $3,248.517 million for total training cost. The cost accounts for differences in training success associated with the scenario's changes in recruit characteristics.

While the same calculation can be applied to the average recruiting cost, we can do better by taking advantage of the RRM in lieu of using the tool's direct calculation for the scenario. The RRM is used to estimate recruiting cost using the same accession requirement and eligibility levels for quality, waivers, and prior service, and making user-specified assumptions about the percentage of the accessions in the year's entry DEP pool, the number of training seats to be filled each month, the end of year DEP goal, and recruiting conditions. The RRM cost is then divided by the number of accessions produced to calculate a per-recruit cost. A second per-recruit cost is added to the RRM estimate based on the cost data provided by HQDA G-1. This second cost was estimated as follows. First, an average cost per recruit for FY15 was estimated with the RRM using the actual FY15 accession production and achieved levels for quality, waivers, and prior service and the actual percentage of the accessions in the year's entry DEP pool, the number of training seats filled each month, end-of-year DEP accomplishment, and FY15 recruiting conditions. The cost estimate per recruit from the RRM was then compared with the G-1's FY15 average cost per recruit. The G-1 cost per recruit was larger, because it includes certain types of costs not covered by the RRM, such as those related to operational costs for recruiters. This difference is treated as an additional cost per recruit. The sum of this per-recruit G-1 cost element and the RRM per-recruit cost estimate is the adjusted estimated cost per recruit for

---

[9] The numbers in Table 3.6 are rounded, and using them may not match the number of accessions needed or the total costs calculated by the tool exactly.

the scenario. It is multiplied by the revised accession goal (using the months-served ratio adjustment, see first paragraph of this section) to generate the adjusted total recruiting cost. The total recruiting cost is then added to the total training cost to estimate the overall total cost for the scenario. Changes in Regular Military Compensation (RMC) costs over the contract term also are considered when the percentage of prior-service recruits is changed.

The total cost estimates produced by the tool including the RRM-based adjustment are shown in Table 3.7.

The cost results shown in Table 3.7 reflect an overall savings in total annual recruiting and training costs of $678 million. However, there is an increase in RMC costs of about $74 million annually. This is based on the greater rank, years of service, and likelihood of being married and having children of the prior-service recruits.[10] The increase

Table 3.7
Tool Total Cost Estimates for Example Scenario (USD, millions)

Outcome	Calculated Baseline	Calculated Excursion
Total accession cost	2,797.041	2,156.839
Total training cost, full	3,541.282	3,499.614
Total training cost, half	3,282.880	3,245.027
Total cost, full	6,338.322	5,656.453
Total cost, half	6,079.920	5,401.866
Change in total accession cost		–640.202
Change in total training cost, full		–41.668
Change in total training cost, half		–37.853
Additional RMC cost for prior-service recruits		73.836
Change in total cost, full		–608.033
Change in total cost, half		–604.218

10 Based on recent data, we estimate the difference in RMC to be about $9,000 annually over the contract term, which we set at an average length of four years. This is calculated

in RMC costs partially offsets the savings in training and recruiting costs, resulting in a net estimated savings of $604 million annually.

Appendix B shows attrition and cost change estimates separately for each of the Tier 2, waiver, and prior-service recruit characteristic levels changed simultaneously above. These results provide insights into the overall effects of the simultaneous changes in the levels of the recruit characteristics. For example, they show that behavioral outcomes, such as attrition rates and costs, can move in different directions. This is because the total savings in recruiting costs from increasing supply can exceed the incremental recruiting and training costs resulting from increased attrition. Or, they can move in the same direction, for example, due to the lower attrition rate and lesser training needs of prior-service recruits. And, as we will discuss again later, it is also important to note that the combination of the recruit selection and RRM tools can generate large differences in potential costs. At the same time, we wish to emphasize that the overall effects of recruit characteristic changes on costs and the optimal enlistment eligibility policy choices very much depend on the size of the recruiting requirement and the difficulty of the recruiting environment.

Summary and Implications

We built a recruit selection tool for the Army to use in assessing the potential effects of rate changes for specific recruit characteristics on outcomes of interest that accounts for the key factors identified in our regression analyses and the covariation among them. The tool allows the user to make simultaneous changes in enlistment cohort representation levels for multiple characteristics. The outcomes include all of the outcomes assessed in the regression analyses plus recruiting cost and numerous training costs.

---

using a pay grade of E-3, one year of service, and single marital status for the first two years and pay grade E-4, three years of service, and married for the last two years for recruits without prior military service. For recruits with prior service, we use E-4, five years of service, and married for the first two years, and E-5, seven years of service, and married with one child for the last two years.

The tool produces a recruiting cost estimate based on information provided annually by HQDA G-1 that uses an average cost per recruit for that year. However, information from the RRM can be incorporated to provide a better estimate that considers changes in recruiting resource requirements per person due to the changes in recruit cohort characteristics, recruiting conditions, and goals the user wishes to assess, in addition to a portion of the G-1 costs not captured in the RRM.

The recruit selection tool also includes a variety of training outcomes: BCT, AIT, OSUT, and IET (covering both basic and occupation training as whole). For each type of training, the training-related outcomes considered include training success or training failure after one try and training success or training failure after multiple tries. The multiple tries are distinguished according to recruits who recycle in the same occupational specialty versus recruits who change their MOS as part of attempting to qualify.

The tool database consists of the characteristics, outcomes, and a set of characteristic weights for each recruit into the Army during FY01–FY11. The user chooses the desired baseline and excursion levels of the recruit characteristics he or she wishes to change. New weights are derived by the tool for each characteristic chosen by the user to produce the new baseline and excursion levels for the characteristics. In addition to examining the prospective effects of changes in enlistment characteristic levels for the cohort as a whole, the tool can be used to investigate the prospective outcomes of changes in recruit characteristics within subgroups. For example, such subgroups could consist of

- recruits with specific characteristics included in the tool
- recruits into specific CMFs/MOSs
- recruits into specific OPAT categories (by using the MOS crosswalk for the OPAT categories).

In this chapter, we illustrated the application of the recruit selection tool to expand supply in challenging recruiting conditions such as those now faced by the Army. We simultaneously varied the representation of four different characteristics in the accession cohort. They are the percentage of (1) Tier 2 (GED) recruits (5 percent to 10 percent), (2) recruits with non-traffic offense enlistment waivers (0 percent to 10 percent), (3) recruits with prior military service (3,000 to 5,000), and (4) AFQT category 1–3A recruits (from 61 percent to 62 percent, reflecting the Army's practice of recruiting a greater rate of AFQT category 1–3As among its Tier 2 recruits). As discussed, these characteristics represent the ones the Army has relied on in the past to increase enlistment supply during difficult recruiting periods. In the illustration, we used the RRM to refine the recruiting cost estimates from those that would be produced by relying simply on the annual cost per recruit information produced historically by HQDA G-1. We used an 80,000 accession requirement, a requirement that the Army found very challenging during the FY06–FY08 period, which, as true today, was characterized by a very low unemployment rate.

The estimated behavioral outcome results reflect limited impact on the rates of adverse outcomes, such as attrition. At the same time, the estimated cost results suggest a large overall savings in total annual recruiting and training cost of $678 million. This savings is driven primarily by a large reduction in estimated recruiting costs due to the increase in supply reflecting the increases in Tier 2, waivered, and prior-service recruits. Because of the increase in recruits with prior military service, RMC costs are estimated to increase by about $74 million annually, due to the prior-service recruits' greater seniority, including their greater rank, years of service, and likelihood of being married and having children. The increase in RMC costs partially offsets the savings in training and recruiting costs, resulting in a net estimated savings of $604 million annually.

The example scenario is helpful in illustrating that using the recruit selection and RRM tools in combination can identify large differences in potential costs and that the estimated effects on outcomes and costs may not move in the same direction. At the same time, it should be noted that the overall effects of recruit characteristic changes on costs and the optimal enlistment eligibility policy choices very much depend on the size of the recruiting requirement and the difficulty of the recruiting environment. Much lower levels of recruiting resources would be needed to meet notably smaller recruiting requirements and/or to meet the Army's recruiting requirements under favorable recruiting conditions, such as periods of high unemployment. In such cases, the savings in recruiting costs from the increase in supply associated with expanding enlistments among Tier 2, waivered, and prior-service recruits would be smaller, and, consequently, its ability to offset increases in recruiting and training costs that could be required by greater attrition and/or poorer performance in training would be reduced.

CHAPTER FOUR

Summary and Conclusions

Successful completion of a recruit's enlistment term is important both to maintain experience and to minimize cost. Recruits who do not complete their first term are unnecessarily expensive because the Army must expend recruiting and IET resources to replace them, while also losing the benefit of their experience. Despite the Army's recent higher levels of beneficial recruit characteristics, such as a lower level of recruits without Tier 1 education credentials or with enlistment waivers, and a future soldier training program, the Army continues to experience its historical first term attrition rate of 30–35 percent. There is a significant body of recruiting research, which includes numerous studies that examine a limited number of predictors of first term success in isolation; however, research that considers how various factors work in combination is necessary to develop more-successful recruit selection tools.

The research described in this report develops a recruit selection tool that estimates a broad range of prospective outcomes and costs for different combinations of recruits' cognitive, noncognitive, demographic, physical, and behavioral attributes. The tool accounts for various combinations of recruit characteristics in predicting soldier success, overall effects on Army loss rates, adverse personnel outcomes, reasons for early separation from the Army, and the costs of alternatives. The tool enables the Army to assess the joint effects of multiple, simultaneous changes in the selection of prospects on losses during the DEP, IET, or the first term; the incidence of outcomes associated with negative personnel flags; adverse reasons for early separation from the Army; and costs. The tool

- can identify combinations of selection rates that will help to minimize attrition during the DEP, IET, and first term, and help the Army minimize other adverse outcomes
- can consider environments requiring increased supply as well as environments in which the eligible recruit pool can be reduced to lower attrition or other problem behaviors
- considers recruiting costs (G-1 and Recruiting Resource Model-based), training costs (BCT, AIT, OSUT, IET, multiple outcomes), and replacement costs and, as appropriate, RMC differences
- can provide insights into large differences in potential costs.

The research proceeded in several steps. First, we reviewed the literature examining (1) the relationship between soldiers' characteristics at enlistment (such as demographic factors, education level and aptitude, physical- and health-related factors, medical and conduct waivers, prior service, test scores) and attrition from the DEP, IET, and their first term, (2) relationships to adverse personnel indicators (such as a bar to reenlistment or a demotion), and (3) reasons for early separation, including those involving conduct or medical reasons. We then integrated these findings.

Using enlistment contract information from the RA Analyst files for FY01–FY11, records from the TAPDB Active Enlisted file for FY01–FY16, and information from the Army Training Requirements and Resources System for the same period, we then quantified the association of each enlistment characteristic identified in the literature separately with DEP, training, and overall first-term attrition. These characteristics included educational attainment, AFQT score, type of waiver, noncognitive/compensatory selection measures (e.g., TTAS, ARMS), BMI/physical condition, time in DEP, prior service, and demographics. In addition to the associations of the individual enlistment characteristics with loss rates in the DEP, IET, or first term, the study team examined the coded reasons for losses. We also analyzed the relationships between enlistment characteristics and adverse outcomes such as a demotion, bar to reenlistment, or a suspension of favorable person status that result in personnel flags in the TAPDB.

Using logistic regression analysis, we then modeled the joint associations of the enlistment characteristics identified individually as the most important predictors with DEP, IET, and first term losses, adverse personnel flag outcomes, and the reasons for early separation, when controlling for recruits' attributes on the other primary characteristics. For each outcome, we examined the extent to which the predictions from the model actually distinguished persons who did well on that outcome from those who fared poorly. The results showed large differences in the actual outcome rates for the recruits predicted to be the low-risk versus high-risk performers. Attrition rates for the lowest-risk quintile of recruits were on the order of 20–30 percentage points lower than those for the high-risk quintile for the failure-to-complete outcomes; 20–35 percentage points lower for the negative personnel flags; and only one-sixth to one-twelfth times as great for each indicated separation reason, a difference of about 4 to 7 percentage points.

Using the factors found to be the primary drivers of the outcomes in the regression results, all else equal, we then built a tool to estimate the prospective effects on outcomes and costs of making single or multiple changes in recruit cohort characteristics. By design, and in distinction from the regressions, the tool allows all of the natural covariation among recruit characteristics to affect the simulation of recruit outcomes and the related costs. As discussed, the outcomes include training performance; DEP, IET, and first-term attrition rates; the rates of adverse personnel flags for a bar to reenlistment, demotion, or suspension of favorable person status; and the rates of specific reasons for early separation. The costs include recruiting, training, and replacement costs, accounting for the number of times recruits attended a training course and the courses attended prior to eventually passing or failing, as well as changes in the number of recruits needed to maintain first term man-months due to changes in attrition associated with the changes in recruit characteristics. Differences in compensation costs associated with these changes also are considered when the number of recruits with prior military service is changed.

Because we want to allow all of the natural covariation among recruit characteristics to affect the simulation of changes in outcomes and the related costs associated with user-specified changes in recruit cohort characteristics, as they would in practice, the quantitative regression results are not used directly by the tool. However, they provide important information in trying to achieve specific objectives concerning for which characteristics to vary enlistment representation and in what direction; which can be changed to increase supply while minimizing potential adverse effects; and, in some cases, concerning which factors might be identifiers for recruit remediation.

In Chapter Three, we discussed application of the recruit selection tool to expand supply in order to help deal with challenging recruiting conditions such as those now faced by the Army. We simultaneously varied the representation of four different characteristics in the accession cohort: the percentage of (1) Tier 2 recruits (5 percent to 10 percent); (2) recruits with non-traffic offense enlistment waivers (0 percent to 10 percent); (3) recruits with prior military service (3,000 to 5,000); and (4) AFQT category 1–3A recruits (from 61 percent to 62 percent, reflecting the Army's practice of recruiting a greater rate of AFQT category 1–3As among its Tier 2 recruits). As discussed, the Army has relied on increasing recruits with these characteristics to increase enlistment supply during difficult recruiting periods in the past. In the illustration, we used the RRM to refine the recruiting cost estimates, rather than relying simply on the annual cost per recruit information produced historically by HQDA G-1. We used an 80,000 accession requirement; the Army found this requirement very challenging to meet during the FY06–FY08 period, which was also characterized by a very low unemployment rate, as is true today.

The estimated behavioral outcome results in the illustration showed limited changes in the rates of adverse outcomes, such as attrition. At the same time, the cost results showed a large estimated overall savings in total annual recruiting and training cost. This savings primarily was the result of a large reduction in estimated recruiting costs associated with the expanded supply of Tier 2, waivered, and prior-service recruits. The prior-service recruits' greater seniority was estimated to increase RMC costs by about $74 million, which caused a limited offset of the savings in training and recruiting cost. The net estimated savings in total cost in the illustration was $604 million annually.

As discussed in Chapter Three and in Appendix B, the example scenario illustrates that the combination of the recruit selection and RRM tools could potentially be very useful to the Army, because the tools can generate large differences in estimated costs. The results also illustrate that the estimated effects of recruit characteristic changes on adverse outcomes and costs can move in parallel, opposite, or unrelated directions. A few comments should be made about these results and about use of the tool more generally.

First, the optimal enlistment eligibility policy choices and the overall effects of recruit characteristic changes on costs depend on recruiting conditions and the magnitude of the recruiting requirement. When recruiting requirements are limited and/or the recruiting environment is favorable, substantially lower levels of recruiting resources are needed. In such situations, the savings in recruiting costs from expanding enlistments among Tier 2, waivered, and prior-service recruits would be smaller. As a result, increases in recruiting and training costs necessitated by greater attrition and/or poorer performance in training would be more difficult to offset.

Second, the possibility of adverse outcomes not directly assessed by the recruit selection tool logically exists. Such outcomes could include changes in job performance, medical problems, or deployability, for example, and their related costs. Addressing such issues directly is beyond the scope of this research; however, the study results provide some related information on outcomes. The outcomes include adverse personnel outcomes, separations for performance reasons, separations for legal reasons, and separations for medical reasons. It should be noted that the two major reasons for non-availability for deployment involve legal and medical issues. It also should be noted that significant differences in rates of outcomes for recruits with specific characteristics, such as those discussed in Chapter Two, do not necessarily translate into large changes in the rates of those outcomes for the accession cohort as a whole. For example, the results in Chapter Two indicate that having a Tier 2 education credential and having a non-traffic offense waiver are each significantly associated with a variety of adverse outcomes. At the same time, however, the illustration in Chapter Three, which increases Tier 2 recruits from 5 percent to 10 percent and simultaneously increases the percentage of recruits with non-traffic offense waivers from 0 percent to 10 percent, shows minimal changes in these types of outcomes. Still, problems that soldiers may experience, such as those of a lesser magnitude, do not always result in personnel flags or separation, so the changes in outcome levels suggested by the tool may understate the full extent of the related issues and fail to capture their costs.

Last, as true for any model or tool, the recruit selection tool's outcomes flow from its underlying database. As discussed, that database includes records for some 870,000 enlisted recruits into the Regular Army between FY01 and FY11. These records provide a great deal of information for a very large number of soldiers. They nonetheless are tied to those soldiers and, thus, have implicit bounds. Running excursions that require significant extrapolation of characteristic levels from those observed over the years covered in the database could produce different outcomes than those suggested by the tool, because the recruits required to achieve such levels may differ in motivation, behavior, or cost from those within the ranges observed.

APPENDIX A

Supplemental Analyses

Tables A.1–A.3 show the means and standard deviations for the predictor variables used in the various analyzes discussed in Chapter Two. Table A.1 pertains to the regressors in the analysis of DEP attrition (Table 2.3). Table A.2 pertains to the regressors in the analysis of IET attrition (Table 2.4). Table A.3 pertains to the regressors in the analyses of first (contract)-term performance; they include:

- Table 2.5. Failure to Complete Term of Service
- Table 2.7. Rank Reduction
- Table 2.8. Bar to Reenlistment
- Table 2.10. Separation for Entry-Level Performance and Conduct
- Table 2.11. Separation for a Physical Condition Other Than a Disability
- Table 2.12. Separation for Failing a Medical or Physical Standard
- Table 2.13. Separation for a Serious Offense
- Table 2.14. Separation for Drug Abuse.

Table A.1
Summary Statistics for Failure to Complete Delayed Entry Program (N = 869,550; loss rate = 12.4 percent)

Variable	Mean	SD
Male	0.8175	0.3863
Age at contract 22–24	0.1663	0.3724
Age at contract 25–30	0.1273	0.3334
Age at contract 31–35	0.0373	0.1894
Age at contract 36+	0.0167	0.1281
Married, kids	0.1237	0.3292
Married, no kids	0.0645	0.2456
Formerly married, kids	0.0108	0.1035
Formerly married, no kids	0.0122	0.1100
Never married, kids	0.0229	0.1497
Asian	0.0311	0.1735
African-American	0.1703	0.3759
Hispanic	0.1061	0.3079
Other non-white non-Hispanic	0.0164	0.1269
Some college	0.0935	0.2911
Four-year college degree	0.0445	0.2063
GED holder	0.1451	0.3522
Traffic offense waiver	0.0029	0.0539
Non-traffic offense waiver	0.0615	0.2403
Drug/alcohol waiver	0.0107	0.1027
Weight waiver	0.0051	0.0715
Other health waiver	0.0067	0.0813
Other non-health waiver	0.0139	0.1169
Scheduled months in DEP	2.4963	3.1223

Table A.1—continued

Variable	Mean	SD
Two-year enlistment	0.0156	0.1239
Three-year enlistment	0.4470	0.4972
Five-year enlistment	0.1004	0.3005
Six-year enlistment	0.0832	0.2762
AFQT categories 1–3A	0.6586	0.4742
Physical capacity = 3	0.0452	0.2077
Upper extremities = 3	0.0073	0.0854
Lower extremities = 3	0.0119	0.1084
Hearing = 3	0.0070	0.0831
Vision = 3	0.0122	0.1099
Psychiatric = 3	0.0212	0.1441
BMI decile 1	0.0943	0.2922
BMI decile 2	0.0944	0.2924
BMI decile 3	0.0944	0.2924
BMI decile 4	0.0942	0.2921
BMI decile 6	0.0939	0.2917
BMI decile 7	0.0936	0.2913
BMI decile 8	0.0939	0.2916
BMI decile 9	0.0945	0.2925
BMI decile 10	0.0934	0.2910
Passed TTAS 112 cutoff	0.3058	0.1308
Took and passed ARMS	0.0048	0.0691
Contract year FY02	0.1139	0.3176
Contract year FY03	0.1029	0.3039
Contract year FY04	0.0845	0.2782
Contract year FY05	0.0849	0.2787

Table A.1—continued

Variable	Mean	SD
Contract year FY06	0.1028	0.3037
Contract year FY07	0.0953	0.2937
Contract year FY08	0.1047	0.3062
Contract year FY09	0.1131	0.3167
Contract year FY10	0.0987	0.2983
Contract month January	0.0822	0.2747
Contract month February	0.0781	0.2683
Contract month March	0.0855	0.2796
Contract month April	0.0811	0.2729
Contract month June	0.0882	0.2835
Contract month July	0.0886	0.2842
Contract month August	0.0954	0.2937
Contract month September	0.0911	0.2878
Contract month October	0.0841	0.2776
Contract month November	0.0741	0.2619
Contract month December	0.0745	0.2626
Prior service	0.0879	0.2831

Table A.2
Summary Statistics for Failure to Complete Initial Entry Training (N = 688,211; loss rate = 12.6 percent)

Variable	Mean	SD
Male	0.8357	0.3706
Age at contract 22–24	0.1606	0.3671
Age at contract 25–30	0.1122	0.3156
Age at contract 31–35	0.0320	0.1761
Age at contract 36+	0.0144	0.1191
Married, kids	0.1069	0.3090
Married, no kids	0.0642	0.2450
Formerly married, kids	0.0095	0.0971
Formerly married, no kids	0.0107	0.1031
Never married, kids	0.0227	0.1491
Asian	0.0321	0.1764
African-American	0.1694	0.3751
Hispanic	0.1077	0.3100
Other non-white non-Hispanic	0.0168	0.1284
Some college	0.0933	0.2909
Four-year college degree	0.0348	0.1832
GED holder	0.1475	0.3546
Traffic offense waiver	0.0031	0.0552
Non-traffic offense waiver	0.0697	0.2546
Drug/alcohol waiver	0.0120	0.1090
Weight waiver	0.0056	0.0743
Other health waiver	0.0078	0.0881
Other non-health waiver	0.0138	0.1168
Scheduled months in DEP	2.4064	2.8677

Table A.2—continued

Variable	Mean	SD
Three-year enlistment	0.4259	0.4945
Five-year enlistment	0.1052	0.3069
Six-year enlistment	0.0912	0.2879
AFQT categories 1–3A	0.6516	0.4765
Physical capacity = 3	0.0366	0.1878
Upper extremities = 3	0.0066	0.0808
Lower extremities = 3	0.0098	0.0986
Hearing = 3	0.0066	0.0811
Vision = 3	0.0122	0.1098
Psychiatric = 3	0.0087	0.0930
BMI decile 1	0.0943	0.2923
BMI decile 2	0.0960	0.2946
BMI decile 3	0.0957	0.2941
BMI decile 4	0.0954	0.2938
BMI decile 6	0.0947	0.2929
BMI decile 7	0.0943	0.2923
BMI decile 8	0.0955	0.2938
BMI decile 9	0.0969	0.2959
BMI decile 10	0.0976	0.2967
Passed TTAS 112 cutoff	0.3061	0.1434
Took and passed ARMS	0.0052	0.0717
Accession year FY02	0.0921	0.2891
Accession year FY03	0.0898	0.2859
Accession year FY04	0.0984	0.2979
Accession year FY05	0.0856	0.2798

Table A.2—continued

Variable	Mean	SD
Accession year FY06	0.0982	0.2976
Accession year FY07	0.0955	0.2939
Accession year FY08	0.0982	0.2976
Accession year FY09	0.0889	0.2846
Accession year FY10	0.0983	0.2977
Accession year FY11	0.0767	0.2660
Accession month January	0.1143	0.3182
Accession month February	0.0791	0.2700
Accession month March	0.0769	0.2665
Accession month April	0.0743	0.2622
Accession month June	0.1007	0.3009
Accession month July	0.1066	0.3086
Accession month August	0.1121	0.3154
Accession month September	0.0858	0.2801
Accession month October	0.0895	0.2855
Accession month November	0.0733	0.2606
Accession month December	0.0125	0.1112
Prior service	0.0515	0.2210

Table A.3
Summary Statistics for First (Contract) Term Outcomes (N = 795,940; loss rate = 34.5 percent)

Variable	Mean	SD
Male	0.8334	0.3726
Age at contract 22–24	0.1704	0.3760
Age at contract 25–30	0.1304	0.3368
Age at contract 31–35	0.0375	0.1899
Age at contract 36+	0.0173	0.1302
Married, kids	0.1237	0.3293
Married, no kids	0.0726	0.2594
Formerly married, kids	0.0107	0.1031
Formerly married, no kids	0.0123	0.1100
Never married, kids	0.0226	0.1486
Asian	0.0318	0.1755
African-American	0.1713	0.3768
Hispanic	0.1064	0.3083
Other non-white non-Hispanic	0.0163	0.1265
Some college	0.0919	0.2888
Four-year college degree	0.0469	0.2115
GED holder	0.1434	0.3504
Traffic offense waiver	0.0027	0.0523
Non-traffic offense waiver	0.0622	0.2415
Drug/alcohol waiver	0.0107	0.1031
Weight waiver	0.0050	0.0707
Other health waiver	0.0072	0.0846
Other non-health waiver	0.0143	0.1185
Scheduled months in DEP	2.3536	2.8794

Table A.3—continued

Variable	Mean	SD
Three-year enlistment	0.4618	0.4985
Five-year enlistment	0.1007	0.3010
Six-year enlistment	0.0862	0.2807
AFQT categories 1–3A	0.6534	0.4759
Physical capacity = 3	0.0371	0.1890
Upper extremities = 3	0.0066	0.0809
Lower extremities = 3	0.0102	0.1005
Hearing = 3	0.0069	0.0830
Vision = 3	0.0126	0.1117
Psychiatric = 3	0.0087	0.0929
BMI decile 1	0.0908	0.2874
BMI decile 2	0.0928	0.2902
BMI decile 3	0.0934	0.2910
BMI decile 4	0.0941	0.2919
BMI decile 6	0.0955	0.2939
BMI decile 7	0.0959	0.2945
BMI decile 8	0.0965	0.2952
BMI decile 9	0.0968	0.2957
BMI decile 10	0.0947	0.2928
Passed TTAS 112 cutoff	0.3058	0.1364
Took and passed ARMS	0.0048	0.0688
Accession year FY02	0.0930	0.2904
Accession year FY03	0.0886	0.2841
Accession year FY04	0.0973	0.2964
Accession year FY05	0.0867	0.2814
Accession year FY06	0.0983	0.2977

Table A.3—continued

Variable	Mean	SD
Accession year FY07	0.0987	0.2983
Accession year FY08	0.0993	0.2991
Accession year FY09	0.0858	0.2801
Accession year FY10	0.0928	0.2901
Accession year FY11	0.0795	0.2705
Accession month January	0.1127	0.3162
Accession month February	0.0818	0.2741
Accession month March	0.0774	0.2672
Accession month April	0.0759	0.2649
Accession month June	0.1008	0.3011
Accession month July	0.1059	0.3077
Accession month August	0.1080	0.3104
Accession month September	0.0839	0.2773
Accession month October	0.0897	0.2858
Accession month November	0.0727	0.2596
Accession month December	0.0164	0.1271
Prior service	0.0955	0.2939

APPENDIX B

Recruit Selection Tool Illustrations

In this appendix, we illustrate the application of the recruit selection tool to assess prospective changes in first-term attrition and the cost associated with expanding supply in challenging recruiting conditions such as those now faced by the Army. We vary the representation of different characteristics in the accession cohort using the same changes discussed in Chapter Three, first individually and then simultaneously. They are the percentage of (1) Tier 2 (GED) recruits, (2) recruits with enlistment waivers,[1] and (3) recruits with prior military service. As discussed earlier, these characteristics represent the ones the Army has most relied on in the past to increase enlistment supply during difficult recruiting periods. As also discussed, the percentage of AFQT category 1–3A recruits covaries with the percentage of Tier 2 recruits, due to the Army's practice of recruiting 80 percent of its Tier 2 recruits from AFQT category 1–3As; this covariation is accounted for explicitly in the excursions in setting the targeted high-quality recruit rate to either 57 percent when the Tier 2 targeted rate is 5 percent or to 54 percent when the Tier 2 targeted rate is 10 percent. In the examples below, we use the RRM to refine the recruiting cost estimates.[2] In these examples, we use an 80,000 accession requirement, a past and possible future

---

[1] To be roughly consistent with past Army practice, we vary the percentage of non-traffic offense waivers from 0 percent to 10 percent, bringing the range of the total waiver rate to 10–20 percent.

[2] As noted earlier, the RRM accounts for the effects of changes in recruiting rates for high-quality, waivered, and prior-service recruits on recruiting costs, subject to the number of enlistment contracts needed and economic conditions.

growth target we wish to illustrate, and assume an unemployment rate of 4.8 percent; the unemployment rate is based on an estimated rate for the FY18–FY19 time frame assuming the current unemployment rate gradually returns to a more average rate. The complete results for all of the outcome measures when the characteristic levels are changed simultaneously are shown in Chapter Three.

To provide insights into the overall effects of the simultaneous changes in the levels of the recruit characteristics listed above, the results presented in this appendix decompose the attrition and cost results for the simultaneous change according to each of the Tier 2, waiver, and prior service characteristics being varied by the user, while holding the other two constant. They illustrate that behavioral outcomes such as attrition rates and cost outcomes can move in different directions or the same direction, that costs can change without much change in attrition, and that the cost changes can be large due to the savings in recruiting costs from increasing supply or the lower attrition rate and lesser training needs of prior-service recruits.

Effects of Increasing Tier 2 Recruits to 10 Percent on Attrition and Cost

As discussed in Chapter Three, the first step is to set the baseline levels for the characteristics of interest that the user wishes to compare the changes to. The baseline levels chosen and discussed in Chapter Three are shown in Table B.1. In the first example, we increase the percentage of Tier 2s in the accession cohort from 5 percent to 10 percent. Table B.1 shows the estimated effects on first-term attrition and cost resulting from this change. As shown in the table, increasing Tier 2 accessions increases the first-term attrition rate by 0.5 percent, from 33.8 percent to 34.3 percent. This increases the number of accessions required to maintain first-term strength. Starting from an 80,000 accession requirement, the average months served in first (contract) term information in the tool output for the baseline and 10 percent Tier 2 cases indicates that the new number of accessions required to generate the same number of man-months is 80,562. The tool also indicates that training costs increase by $13.5 million annually, due to the larger number of recruits required and differences in training performance associated with the different mix of recruits with respect to the higher level of Tier 2 recruits. However, the cost results shown in Table B.1 reflect a *savings* of $193 million in total annual cost. This indicates that the lower recruiting cost for Tier 2 youth more than offsets the effects of the increase in accessions needed and the costs associated with differences in training outcomes. This is an example of reducing cost through enlistment cohort characteristic changes despite increased attrition.

Effects of Increasing Enlistment Waivers to 20 Percent on Attrition and Cost

In the second example, we increase the percentage of recruits with enlistment waivers for non-traffic legal offenses from 0 percent to 10 percent, raising the total waiver rate from 10 percent to 20 percent. Table B.2 shows the estimated effects on first-term attrition and cost resulting from this change. As shown in the table, increasing the percentage of recruits with non-traffic legal offense waivers to 10 percent has little effect on the first-term attrition rate, from 33.8 percent to 33.7 percent. There is a slight increase in the number of accessions required to maintain first-term strength, due to a small decrease in

Table B.1
Simulated Effects on First-Term Attrition and Cost of Increasing Tier 2 Recruits

Characteristic and Value	Attrition	Cost (Millions)
Baseline (5% Tier 2)	33.8%	6,080
10% Tier 2	34.3%	5,887

NOTES: Baseline: 5% Tier 2, 10% waivers, 3,000 prior service, 61% AFQT category 1–3A, 17% Hispanic. Excursion: 10% Tier 2, 10% waivers, 3,000 prior service, 62% AFQT category 1–3A, 17% Hispanic. Cost includes training costs and recruiting costs, which can vary with recruit characteristics.

Table B.2
Simulated Effects on First-Term Attrition and Cost of Increasing Recruits with Non-Traffic Legal Offense Waivers

Characteristic and Value	Attrition	Cost (Millions)
Baseline (10% Waivers)	33.8%	6,080
20% Waivers	33.7%	5,736

NOTES: Baseline: 5% Tier 2, 10% waivers, 3,000 prior service, 61% AFQT category 1–3A, 17% Hispanic. Excursion: 5% Tier 2, 20% waivers, 3,000 prior service, 61% AFQT category 1–3A, 17% Hispanic. Cost includes training costs and recruiting costs, which can vary with recruit characteristics.

the average months served in the term, from 36.3 to 36.2 months. Starting from an 80,000 accession requirement, the average-months-served information in the tool output for the baseline and 10 percent non-traffic legal offense waiver cases indicates that the new number of accessions required to generate the same number of man-months is 80,241. The tool also indicates that training costs increase by $3.7 million annually, due to the slightly larger number of recruits required and differences in training performance associated with the different mix of recruits with respect to the higher level of waivered recruits. The cost results shown in Table B.2 reflect an overall savings in total annual cost of $344 million, however. This indicates that the lower recruiting cost from expanding eligibility for waivered recruits more than offsets the effects of the increase in accessions needed and the costs associated with differences in training outcomes.

Effects of Increasing Recruits with Prior Military Service to 5,000 on Attrition and Cost

In the third example, we increase the number of recruits with prior military service from 3,000 to 5,000. Table B.3 shows the estimated effects on first-term attrition and cost resulting from this change. As shown in the table, increasing the number of recruits with prior service to 5,000 reduces the first-term attrition rate from 33.8 percent to 33.5 percent. There is nonetheless a very slight increase in the number of accessions required to maintain first-term strength, due to a small decrease (0.016 months) in the average months served in the term. Starting from an 80,000 accession requirement, the average-months-served information in the tool output for the baseline and 5,000 prior-service cases indicates that the new number of accessions required to generate the same number of man-months is 80,035. The slight increase in recruits required despite the somewhat lower attrition rate can be attributed to the fact that average term length is shorter for prior-service recruits. The tool also indicates that training costs decrease substantially by $53.1 million annually; this is because most prior-service recruits do not need to repeat basic training, and many also do not need to repeat MOS training. The cost results shown in Table B.3 reflect an overall savings in total annual recruiting and training cost of $139 million. However, as indicated in the note the table, there is an increase in RMC costs of about $74 million annually. This is based on the greater rank, years of service, and likelihood of being married and having children among prior-service recruits. The increase in RMC costs partially

Table B.3
Simulated Effects on First-Term Attrition and Cost of Increasing Recruits with Prior Military Service

Characteristic and Value	Attrition	Cost (Millions)
Baseline (500 Prior Service)	33.8%	6,080
5,000 Prior Service	33.5%	6,015

NOTES: Baseline: 5% Tier 2, 10% waivers, 3,000 prior service, 61% AFQT category 1–3A, 17% Hispanic. Excursion: 5% Tier 2, 10% waivers, 5,000 prior service, 61% AFQT category 1–3A, 17% Hispanic. Cost includes training costs and recruiting costs, which can vary with recruit characteristics. RMC costs are estimated to increase by $74 million due to the increase in accessions with prior military service.

offsets the savings in training costs, resulting in a net estimated savings of $65 million annually.[3]

Effects of Simultaneously Increasing Tier 2, Waivered, and Prior-Service Recruits on Attrition and Cost

The fourth example is analogous to the one discussed in Chapter Three. Here, we simultaneously increase the percentage of Tier 2 recruits (5 percent to 10 percent), waivered recruits (10 percent to 20 percent), and recruits with prior military service (3,000 to 5,000). Table B.4 shows the estimated effects on first-term attrition and cost resulting from this change. As shown in the table, making these changes is estimated to have a small effect on the first-term attrition rate, increasing it by less than 0.1 percentage points (from 33.781 percent to 33.849 percent).

Table B.4
Simulated Effects on First-Term Attrition and Cost of Simultaneously Increasing Tier 2, Waivered, and Prior-Service Recruits

Characteristic and Value	Attrition	Cost (Millions)
Baseline	33.8%	6,080
Full excursion	33.8%	5,476

NOTES: Baseline: 5% Tier 2, 10% waivers, 3,000 prior service, 61% AFQT category 1–3A, 17% Hispanic. Excursion: 10% Tier 2, 20% waivers, 5,000 prior service, 62% AFQT category 1–3A, 17% Hispanic. Cost includes training costs and recruiting costs, which can vary with recruit characteristics. RMC costs are estimated to increase by $74 million due to the increase in accessions with prior military service.

---

[3] As discussed earlier, based on recent data, we estimate the difference in RMC to be about $9,000 annually over the first term, which we set at an average length of four years. This is calculated using a pay grade of E-3, one year of service, and single marital status for the first two years and pay grade E-4, three years of service, and married for the last two years for recruits without prior military service. For recruits with prior service, we use E-4, five years of service, and married for the first two years, and E-5, seven years of service, and married with one child for the last two years.

This increases the number of accessions required to maintain first-term strength. Starting from an 80,000 accession requirement, the average-months-served information in the tool output for the baseline and full excursion cases indicates that the new number of accessions required to generate the same number of man-months increases to 80,759. The tool also indicates, however, that training costs decrease by $37.9 million annually, due to the much smaller training requirements of prior-service recruits, as well as differences in training performance associated with the different mix of recruits. The cost results shown in Table B.4 reflect a decrease in overall total annual recruiting and training costs of about $678 million. This savings is partially offset by the increase in RMC for the larger number of recruits with prior military service. The net effect is estimated to be a decrease in overall costs of about $604 million annually. This is another example of reducing cost through enlistment cohort characteristic changes despite a limited effect on attrition.

APPENDIX C

Use of Recruit Selection Tool

As discussed, the recruit selection tool is designed to estimate the prospective effects of changing the levels of specific characteristics of the enlistment cohort on outcomes of interest to the Army. This includes behavioral outcomes and costs. This appendix describes how to use the tool. It sets the user-supplied values in the tool to those for the excursion discussed in Chapter Three.

To run the tool, the user must have a recent version of R and install the following packages: foreign, gtools, shiny, xlsx, and xtable. Unless there are restrictions on access to the Internet (whether through lack of access or due to a firewall), the R script is install.packages. R will take care of this; the user should simply copy and paste the code into the R console. The user may be asked to select a Comprehensive R Archive Network (CRAN) repository to install the packages from; choose the closest site geographically (e.g., USA1 Berkeley). In addition to R, the user may download RStudio or any other R graphical user interface (GUI) to access the code. Finally, depending on whether or not the user uses RStudio, a recent version of any popular web browser may also be needed (Internet Explorer, Chrome, Firefox, etc.). Internet access is not required once R, RStudio, and the packages have been downloaded.

There are three ways to access the tool. First, to access the tool using the run.bat file located in the app folder, the user will need to use a Windows operating system and have a web browser. In this case, the user can simply double click run.bat. The tool will open automatically in the user's default web browser after a short load time. Second, to access the tool on a Macintosh without RStudio, the user will need to open the runApp.R file (also located in the app folder) in R and then source (or copy/paste) the script to the R console. The final, third method requires RStudio but works for both Windows and Macintosh operating systems. The user should open the file app.R in RStudio (also located in the app folder), and in the top right corner where app.R appears there should be a button that says "Run App"; click this button, and, depending on the selected options, the tool will open in a new window or in the user's default browser.

Once the tool has loaded, on the left side of the screen there will be a side panel for inputs; the right side will list a few titles for outputs. Screenshots of the tool GUI are shown in Figures C.1–C.3.

Step 1

The first step is to select the sample to be included in the desired analysis. The user must select which point in the enlistment cycle he or she would like to explore: all enlistees (including those in the DEP waiting to access) or just those who have accessed onto active duty (which will limit the sample to those who completed the DEP). There also are additional options to focus on other subsamples for the recruits who accessed. These additional options include selecting recruits who took specific types of training courses (BCT, AIT, OSUT) in order to focus on outcomes during those training courses, subsampling to focus on training as a whole (IET), or focusing on recruits' post-training in-unit outcomes. In addition, the user also can limit the sample to focus on prospective outcomes for recruits falling into specific Occupational Physical Assessment Test (OPAT) categories by unchecking the other categories. (The default setting includes all soldiers.) The three OPAT categories are heavy, significant, and moderate. Recruits are categorized using their MOS and a crosswalk of the specific MOSs associated with each OPAT category. The crosswalk is shown in Table C.1.[1] Once

1 We were unable to place 27,143 recruits into one of the OPAT categories based on the MOS information contained in their enlistment records. This amounts to 3.4 percent of the accessions.

the sample has been selected, the user should press the "Select Data" button before moving on to Step 2.

Step 2

After selecting the desired sample, the user selects the number of recruit characteristics that he or she wishes to weight in order to create a new baseline case for comparison purposes or an excursion from that new baseline. The user interface limits the number of characteristics that can be simultaneously selected for weighting to between one and six. The program underlying the tool can simultaneously weight all of the characteristics in the database (see Table 3.1). Thus, the GUI could be altered to allow more than six characteristics to be weighted simultaneously. However, the computation time required to calculate the weighted results increases at a factorial rate. For this reason, we believe it becomes undesirable to weight more than six characteristics simultaneously. A six-characteristic run takes approximately two and one-half hours to complete; therefore, a seven-characteristic run would require between 17 and 18 hours. In contrast, runs involving five characteristics take about 25 minutes, depending on the computer's speed; runs weighting four characteristics simultaneously, only about five minutes; runs involving three characteristics, just over one minute; and those involving weighting one or two characteristics require less than one minute to complete. The example in Figure C.1 weights five recruit characteristics simultaneously.

If desired, the user can focus on other subsets of the database—for example, recruits into specific MOSs, such as combat MOSs. This is done by limiting the recruits in the final_data_5603_for_app.dta file within the dta folder to the subset of interest; renaming the subset file to a name of the user's choosing, and then editing line 263 of the tool program code from: MAINDATA <-read.dta("dta/final_data_5603_for_app.dta") to use the new data file name.

Figure C.1
Recruit Selection Tool Interface, Steps 1–3

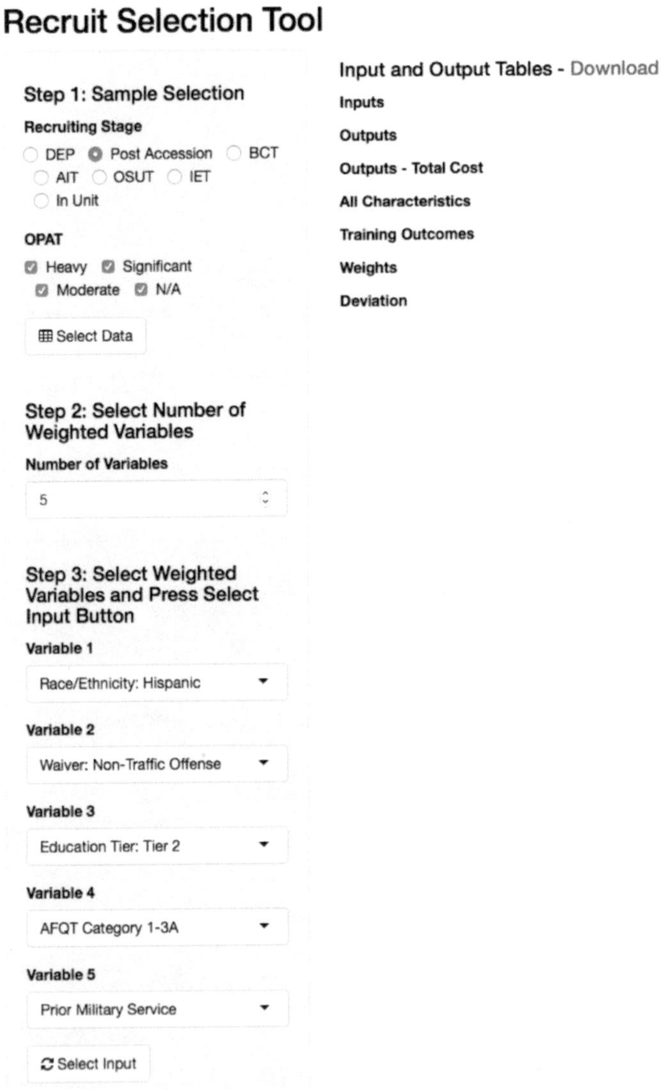

RAND *RR2267-C.1*

Table C.1
OPAT Category—MOS Crosswalk

Heavy						
11B	11C	11X	12B	12C	12D	12P
13B	13F	15V	15Y	18B	18C	18D
18E	18F	18X	19D	19K	88H	88K
88M	92M					
Significant						
12G	12M	12V	14P	14S	15B	15D
15E	15F	15J	15N	15R	15S	15T
15U	15W	25L	25R	31B	31K	42A
42R	42S	68W	88L	88N	92A	92F
92G	92R	92S	92W			
Moderate						
00Z	09B	09C	09D	09E	09J	09L
09M	09N	09Q	09R	09S	09T	09U
09W	11Z	12A	12H	12K	12N	12Q
12R	12T	12W	12X	12Y	12Z	13D
13J	13M	13P	13R	13T	13X	13Z
14E	14G	14H	14T	14X	14Z	15G
15H	15K	15L	15P	15Q	15Z	17C
18Z	19Z	25B	25C	25D	25E	25M
25N	25P	25Q	25S	25T	25U	25V
25W	25X	25Z	27D	29E	31D	31E
35F	35G	35L	35M	35N	35P	35Q
35S	35T	35V	35X	35Y	35Z	36B
37F	38B	46Q	46R	46Z	51C	56M
68A	68B	68C	68D	68E	68F	68G
68H	68J	68K	68L	68M	68N	68P
68Q	68R	68S	68T	68U	68V	68X
68Y	68Z	74D	79R	79S	79T	79V
88U	88Z	89A	89B	89D	91A	91B
91C	91D	91E	91F	91G	91H	91J
91L	91M	91P	91S	91X	91Z	92L
92Y	92Z	94A	94D	94E	94F	94H
94M	94P	94R	94S	94T	94W	94Y
94Z						

Step 3

Any of the recruit characteristics shown earlier in Table 3.1 can be selected for weighting to establish a new baseline for comparison purposes or a new excursion scenario from that baseline. It is important to keep in mind that the database includes soldiers who accessed between FY01 and FY11. Consequently, the historical levels of some recruit characteristics across the entire database can differ from their more recent levels. For this reason, establishing new baseline levels for the characteristics the user wishes to explore changing in an excursion scenario is a desirable first step. In the example provided, we applied a weight for Hispanic recruits to account for the recent increase in the percentage of such recruits. After selecting the characteristics to weight, the user must click "Select Input."

In selecting the characteristics to be weighted and their weights, the user should consider the nature of the excursion he or she wishes to run. This involves whether the user wishes to assess (1) the full effects of changing the levels of the multiple characteristics being weighted, (2) their independent effects, or (3) whether the purpose is to examine the prospective effects of changes in the level of each of the characteristics being weighted in the excursion scenario when letting all of the covariation between that characteristic and other recruit characteristics influence the estimated changes in behavioral outcomes and costs. We expect that the user would normally want to perform the first of these three types of assessments. It is possible, though, that the user may wish to explore the independent effects of the recruit characteristics he or she is changing. In this case, the user would specify the new targeted characteristic level in the excursion scenario for each of the characteristics being changed one at a time, while specifying the new baseline targeted levels for the others. We discussed this type of analysis at length in Appendix B. In the third case, the user would choose one (or a subset) of the characteristics being weighted in the excursion using the target level(s). The tool would then allow the other characteristic levels to float from their new baseline levels. In the second and third cases, the user should select "Use Updated Characteristics as New Baseline" in Step 6. This is discussed below.

Step 4

In Step 4, the user uses the sliding bars to set the targeted characteristic level in the new baseline or excursion scenario for each of the characteristic levels being changed. If the level of recruits with prior military service is being varied, it is entered as a percentage of the accession goal specified in Step 5. If the number of months scheduled in the DEP is being varied, the targeted value is entered with up to one decimal place. See Figure C.2.

Step 5

The user also must indicate the Army's accession goal for the year of analysis. This number is used as one of the inputs in determining the number of accessions to cost for training and recruiting cost estimates. If the user wishes to use an RRM-adjusted cost for the recruiting cost calculation, which is recommended, as discussed earlier, then this cost also must be input. Last, if the RRM-adjusted cost estimate is being used and the results for a baseline and excursion scenario are being compared, then, if they differ from one another, the numbers of prior-service recruits used in the RRM-adjusted costs for the baseline and excursion scenarios must be entered. The tool then calculates the difference in estimated RMC cost for the excursion versus the baseline scenario.

Step 6

The final user input involves specifying which values to use for the starting point for the new run. There are three choices, based on what the user wants to do. If the purpose is simply to run an excursion from the historical FY01–FY11 recruit database with specific targeted levels for some of the characteristics, then the user would select "Use Historical Characteristics." If, however, the user also plans to use that excursion as a new baseline to compare other excursions against, then the

Figure C.2
Recruit Selection Tool Interface, Steps 4–5

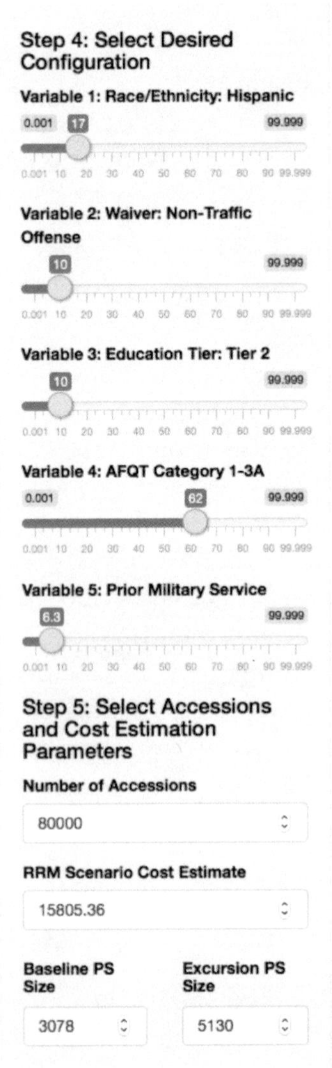

RAND *RR2267-C.2*

Figure C.3
Recruit Selection Tool Interface, Step 6

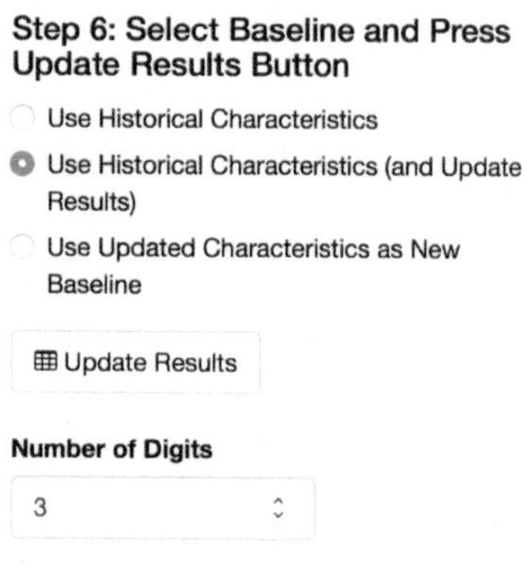

RAND *RR2267-C.3*

user would select "Use Historical Characteristics and Update Results." Last, if the user now wants to run such an excursion against the new baseline, then he or she would select "Use Updated Characteristics as New Baseline." The user then clicks the "Update Results" button. The user does not need to regenerate the baseline between each excursion scenario as long as the tool remains open. Finally, there is an option to select the number of digits to the right of the decimal point the user wishes to see in the output. This can be changed after the calculations have been performed.

Outcomes Generated

Several types of results are stored from each tool run. They include the final weight applied to each row (soldier) in the database when generating a new baseline or excursion case.[2] At the top of the screen of outcomes, there will appear a string of text that starts "Sequential

---

[2] In subsequent runs, the stored weight can be applied to each soldier at the beginning of a new excursion.

outcome with the smallest deviation." This indicates the order in which the weights were applied in order to most closely match the targeted levels in the baseline or excursion. The order for the excursion presented in Chapter Three is non-traffic offense waiver, AFQT category 1–3A, Tier 2, prior service, Hispanic.

Next, there is a summary table of the inputs selected. This table shows all the characteristics selected for weighting, their historical percentages, their target values selected by the user, and their "sequential" value (their value produced by the tool when optimizing the weighting sequence to most closely produce the targeted values for the characteristics selected by the user). See Tables 3.3–3.5 in Chapter Three.

The second table produced is a summary of the outputs. It includes all of the outputs shown in Table 3.2, except for those pertaining to total cost.[3] See Table 3.6. The third table contains the total costs. See Table 3.7. While the second output table shows the average cost of a recruit and trainee for the run, the total cost table calculates the total cost based on the accession goal, the change in months served during the first term (using the ratio procedure described earlier to adjust required accessions), the RRM-adjusted per recruit cost estimate (see Chapter Three), and a RMC adjustment if the percentage of recruits with prior military service is changed.

The fourth table shows the new levels for all of the recruit characteristics in Table 3.1, both those weighted in the run those not weighted. These results for the baseline and excursion discussed in Chapter Three are shown in Table C.2.

Table C.3 breaks out outcomes for the individual types of training for the Chapter Three baseline and excursion. This includes the percentage of soldiers who passed a given training component on the first try, who passed after multiple tries, who failed on the first try (without taking the course again), or who failed after multiple tries (never succeeding in passing the course).

---

3 The exception to this is when the DEP sample has been selected. Recruits who do not access have no data on most outcomes. For this sample, we show only the DEP loss percentage.

Table C.2
Results for Recruit Characteristics

Characteristic	Baseline	Excursion
Female	18.588	17.010
Age at contract: 17–21	68.965	65.583
Age at contract: 22–24	15.830	16.998
Age at contract: 25–30	10.975	12.465
Age at contract: 31–35	2.992	3.452
Age at contract: 36 and above	1.176	1.443
Marital and children status: married, kids	10.178	11.507
Marital and children status: married, no kids	6.676	6.929
Marital and children status: formerly married, kids	0.804	0.981
Marital and children status: formerly married, no kids	1.011	1.110
Marital and children status: never married, kids	2.069	2.319
Marital and children status: never married, no kids	79.262	77.154
Race/Ethnicity: white, non-Hispanic	60.266	61.792
Race/Ethnicity: African-American	17.104	16.260
Race/Ethnicity: Hispanic	17.341	17.000
Race/Ethnicity: Asian	3.246	3.018
Race/Ethnicity: other non-white non-Hispanic	1.633	1.555
Education: some college	10.173	9.784
Education: 4-year college degree	4.866	4.596
Traffic offense waiver	0.324	0.276
Non-traffic offense waiver	0.001	10.020
Drug/alcohol waiver	1.132	1.015
Weight waiver	0.579	0.507
Health condition waiver (PULHES ≠ 3)	0.857	0.733
Other waiver	1.630	1.428

Table C.2—continued

Characteristic	Baseline	Excursion
2-year term	1.336	1.338
3-year term	43.341	45.397
4-year term	35.814	35.040
5-year term	10.746	9.881
6-year term	8.762	8.344
Tier 2	4.961	9.911
AFQT categories 1–3A	61.000	62.011
Physical capacity = 3	3.766	3.528
Upper extremities = 3	0.672	0.634
Lower extremities = 3	1.007	0.960
Hearing = 3	0.655	0.641
Vision = 3	1.366	1.239
Psychiatric = 3	0.827	0.816
BMI: 1st decile	9.200	8.970
BMI: 2nd decile	9.343	9.219
BMI: 3rd decile	9.415	9.335
BMI: 4th decile	9.512	9.430
BM: 5th decile	9.538	9.484
BMI: 6th decile	9.636	9.622
BMI: 7th decile	9.556	9.609
BMI: 8th decile	9.529	9.738
BMI: 9th decile	9.617	9.780
BMI: 10th decile	9.735	9.695
BMI: Missing	4.919	5.118
Accession month: January	11.005	11.283
Accession month: February	8.016	8.199

Table C.2—continued

Characteristic	Baseline	Excursion
Accession month: March	7.440	7.688
Accession month: April	7.196	7.528
Accession month: May	7.172	7.398
Accession month: June	10.756	10.122
Accession month: July	11.403	10.734
Accession month: August	11.145	10.901
Accession month: September	8.391	8.424
Accession month: October	8.918	8.953
Accession month: November	7.132	7.255
Accession month: December	1.427	1.515
TTAS score ≥ 112 (takers)	30.538	30.568
TTAS non-takers	96.313	93.224
Took and passed ARMS	0.499	0.505
Prior service	3.707	6.300
Months scheduled in DEP	2.665	2.418
Accession year: 2001	7.482	7.234
Accession year: 2002	9.570	9.413
Accession year: 2003	9.495	9.127
Accession year: 2004	10.394	9.923
Accession year: 2005	8.408	8.627
Accession year: 2006	8.671	9.608
Accession year: 2007	8.313	9.566
Accession year: 2008	8.789	9.687
Accession year: 2009	8.716	8.750
Accession year: 2010	10.655	9.673
Accession year: 2011	9.508	8.394

Table C.3
Detailed Training Results

Outcome by Training Type	Baseline	Excursion
Passed AIT on first try	84.442	84.501
Passed AIT on multiple tries	8.962	8.853
Failed AIT on first try	4.007	4.044
Failed AIT on multiple tries	2.590	2.602
Passed BCT on first try	90.516	90.608
Passed BCT on multiple tries	2.060	2.054
Failed BCT on first try	6.954	6.880
Failed BCT on multiple tries	0.470	0.458
Passed IET on first try	79.567	79.757
Passed IET on multiple tries	8.088	8.011
Failed IET on first try	10.155	10.056
Failed IET on multiple tries	2.190	2.175
Passed OSUT on first try	85.209	85.079
Passed OSUT on multiple tries	3.717	3.849
Failed OSUT on first try	10.147	10.140
Failed OSUT on multiple tries	0.926	0.932

The two final tables contain weight-related details. They report the weights derived by the tool to meet the targeted value for each of the characteristic levels being changed in the run (Table C.4) prior to the weight iteration process, as well as the absolute value of the percentage point deviation of the final value for each weighted characteristic level from its targeted value (Table C.5).

Table C.4
Characteristic Weights for Target Levels

Characteristic	Weight
Hispanic = 1	1.596
Hispanic = 0	0.929
Non-Traffic Offense Waiver = 1	1.594
Non-Traffic Offense Waiver = 0	0.960
Tier 2 = 1	0.705
Tier 2 = 0	1.049
AFQT category 1–3A = 1	0.944
AFQT category 1–3A = 0	1.107
Prior Service = 1	0.667
Prior Service = 0	1.035

Table C.5
Deviation of Calculated from Targeted Characteristic Values for Excursion

Deviation Type	Percentage Points
Total sum	0.120
Hispanic	0.000
Non-traffic offense waiver	0.020
Tier 2	0.089
AFQT category 1–3A	0.011
Prior service	0.000

Bibliography

Allison, Stephen C., Marilyn A. Sharp, and Joseph J. Knapik, *Predictive Models to Estimate Probabilities of Injuries and Adverse Performance Outcomes in U.S. Army Basic Combat Training*, Natick, Mass.: U.S. Army Research Institute of Environmental Medicine, USARIEM Technical Report T14-3, March 2014.

Andrew, John J., *Improved Screening for Navy Enlistment*, master's thesis, Monterey, Calif.: Naval Postgraduate School, March 2009.

Asonye, Chinomso Elvy, *Analysis of Body Mass Index and First-Term Attrition of Navy Enlisted Personnel*, master's thesis, Monterey, Calif.: Naval Postgraduate School, June 2017.

Bartone, P. T., R. R. Roland, J. J. Picano, and T. J. Williams, "Psychological Hardiness Predicts Success in US Army Special Forces Candidates," *International Journal of Selection & Assessment*, Vol. 16, No. 1, 2008.

Baykiz, Murat Sami, *An Analysis of Marine Corps Delayed Entry Program (DEP) Attrition by High School Graduates and High School Seniors*, master's thesis, Monterey, Calif.: Naval Postgraduate School, March 2007.

Beal, Scott A., *The Roles of Perseverance, Cognitive Ability, and Physical Fitness in U.S. Army Special Forces Assessment and Selection*, Arlington, Va.: U.S. Army Research Institute for the Behavioral and Social Sciences, Research Report 1927, 2010. As of November 3, 2017:
http://dtic.mil/dtic/tr/fulltext/u2/a525579.pdf

Bedno, Sheryl A., Christine E. Lang, William E. Daniell, Andrew R. Wiesen, Bennett Datu, and David W. Niebuhr, "Association of Weight at Enlistment with Enrollment in the Army Weight Control Program and Subsequent Attrition in the Assessment of Recruit Motivation and Strength," *Military Medicine*, Vol. 175, No. 3, March 2010, pp. 1–6.

Bedno, Sheryl A., Yuanzhang Li, Weiwei Han, David N. Cowan, Christine T. Scott, Melinda A. Cavicchia, and David W. Niebuhr, "Exertional Heat Illness Among Overweight U.S. Army Recruits in Basic Training," *Aviation, Space, and Environmental Medicine*, Vol. 81, No. 2, February 2010, pp. 107–111.

Buddin, Richard, *Success of First-Term Soldiers: The Effects of Recruiting Practices and Recruit Characteristics*, Santa Monica, Calif.: RAND Corporation, MG-262-A, 2005. As of November 3, 2017: https://www.rand.org/pubs/monographs/MG262.html

Campbell, J. P., and L. M. Zook, *Building and Retaining the Career Force: New Procedures for Accessing and Assigning Army Enlisted Personnel—Final Report*, Arlington, Va.: U.S. Army Research Institute for the Behavioral and Social Sciences, 1996.

Carroll, James M., *Study of Navy Enlisted Attrition: Race, Ethnicity, and Type of Occupation*, master's thesis, Monterey, Calif.: Naval Postgraduate School, September 2008.

Cortina, J. M., M. L. Doherty, N. Schmitt, G. Kaufman and R. G. Smith, "The 'Big Five' Personality Factors in the IPI and MMPI: Predictors of Police Performance," *Personnel Psychology*, Vol. 45, No. 1, 1992, pp. 119–140.

Cox, Karin A., Kathryn L. Clark, Yuanzhang Li, Timothy E. Powers, and Margot R. Krauss, "Prior Knee Injury and Risk of Future Hospitalization and Discharge from Military Service," *American Journal of Preventive Medicine*, Vol. 18, No. 3 Suppl., 2000, pp. 112–117.

Department of Defense Instruction 3216.02, *Protection of Human Subjects and Adherence to Ethical Standards in DoD-Supported Research*, Washington, D.C.: U.S. Department of Defense, November 8, 2011.

Distifeno, Christopher, *Effects of Moral Conduct Waivers on First-term Attrition of U.S. Army Soldiers*, master's thesis, Monterey, Calif.: Naval Postgraduate School, March 2008.

Eubanks, Lee H., "Navy Recruit Attrition Prediction Modeling," master's thesis, Monterey, Calif.: Naval Postgraduate School, September 2014.

Fischl, M. A., and D. L. Blackwell, *Attrition in the Army from the Signing of the Enlistment Contract Through 180 Days of Service*, Arlington, Va.: U.S. Army Research Institute for the Behavioral and Social Sciences, 2000.

Golfin, Peggy A., with Lynda G. Houck, *Effectiveness of the Hp3 Screen for Non-High-School-Diploma Graduates: Was FY01 a Better Year?* Alexandria, Va.: CNA, D0005438.A2, February 2002.

Greenamyer, Darren H., *Study of Enlistment Test Scores and Other Attrition Factors from the Navy's Delayed Entry Program*, master's thesis, Monterey, Calif.: Naval Postgraduate School, March 2009. As of November 3, 2017: http://www.dtic.mil/dtic/tr/fulltext/u2/a496769.pdf

Greenston, P. M., *The Optimal Job-Person Match Case for Attrition Reduction*, Arlington, Va.: U.S. Army Research Institute for the Behavioral and Social Sciences, 1997.

Hartmann, Ellen, and Cato Gronnerod, "Rorschach Variables and Big Five Scales as Predictors of Military Training Completion: A Replication Study of the Selection of Candidates to the Naval Special Forces in Norway," *Journal of Personality Assessment*, Vol. 91, No. 3, 2009, pp. 254–264.

Hunter, Arwen, Leonard White, and Mark Young, "Predicting First-Term Enlisted Attrition: The Tier Two Attrition Screen," paper presented at meeting of the American Psychological Association, Boston, Mass., 2008.

Huth, Richard A., *The Effect of Moral Waivers on the Success of Navy Recruits*, master's thesis, Monterey, Calif.: Naval Postgraduate School, September 2007.

Jeppe, Adam L., *Determining the Relationship Between Moral Waivers and Marine Corps Unsuitability Attrition*, master's thesis, Monterey, Calif.: Naval Postgraduate School, March 2008.

Knapik, J. J., K. G. Hauret, J. L. Lange, and B. Jovag, "Retention in Service of Recruits Assigned to the Army Physical Fitness Test Enhancement Program in Basic Combat Training," *Military Medicine*, Vol. 168, No. 6, 2003.

Knapp, David, Bruce R. Orvis, Christopher E. Maerzluft, and Tiffany Tsai, *Resources Required to Meet Army's Enlisted Recruiting Requirements Under Alternative Recruiting Goals, Conditions, and Eligibility Policies*, Santa Monica, Calif.: RAND Corporation, forthcoming.

Knapp, Deirdre J., and Tonia S. Heffner, eds., *Expanded Enlistment Eligibility Metrics (EEEM): Recommendations on a Non-Cognitive Screen for New Soldier Selection*, Arlington, Va.: U.S. Army Research Institute for the Behavioral and Social Sciences, 2010.

Knapp, Deirdre J., and Kate A. LaPort, eds., *Tier One Performance Screen Initial Operational Test and Evaluation: 2012 Annual Report*, Arlington, Va.: U.S. Army Research Institute for the Behavioral and Social Sciences, 2014.

Loughran, David S., and Bruce R. Orvis, *The Effect of the Assessment of Recruit Motivation and Strength (ARMS) Program on Army Accessions and Attrition*, Santa Monica, Calif.: RAND Corporation, TR-975-A, 2011. As of November 3, 2017: https://www.rand.org/pubs/technical_reports/TR975.html

Malone, Lauren, and Neil Carey, with Yevgeniya Pinelis and Dave Gregory, *Waivered Recruits: An Evaluation of Their Performance and Attrition Risk*, Alexandria, Va.: CNA, D0023955.A4, March 2011. AS of November 3, 2017: https://www.cna.org/CNA_files/PDF/D0023955.A4.pdf

Niebuhr, David W., Yuanzhang Li, Timothy E. Powers, Margot R. Krauss, David Chandler, and Thomas Heifer, "Attrition of U.S. Military Enlistees with Waivers for Hearing Deficiency, 1995–2004," *Military Medicine*, Vol. 172, No. 1, 2007, pp. 63–69. As of November 3, 2017:
http://www.amsara.amedd.army.mil/Documents/AMSARA%20Publication/17-Niebuhr-Jan-2007.pdf

Niebuhr, David W., Timothy E. Powers, Yuanzhang Li, and Amy M. Millikan, "Morbidity and Attrition Related to Medical Conditions in Recruits," Chapter 4 in Bernard L. DeKoning, ed., *The Textbook of Military Medicine: Recruit Medicine*, Silver Spring, Md.: Walter Reed Army Institute of Research, Accession Medical Standards Analysis and Research Activity (AMSARA), 2006, pp. 59–79. As of November 3, 2017:
http://www.amsara.amedd.army.mil/Documents/AMSARA%20Publication/17_Niebuhr_RecruitMedicine_2006.pdf

Niebuhr, David W., Christine T. Scott, Yuanzhang Li, Sheryl A. Bedno, Han, Weiwei Han, and Timothy E. Powers, "Preaccession Fitness and Body Composition as Predictors of Attrition in U.S. Army Recruits," *Military Medicine*, Vol. 174, No. 7, July 2009, pp. 695–701.

Nye, Christopher D., Fritz Drasgow, Oleksandr S. Chernyshenko, Stephen Stark, U. Christean Kubisiak, Leonard A. White, and Irwin Jose, *Assessing the Tailored Adaptive Personality Assessment System*, Fort Belvoir, Va.: U.S. Army Research Institute for the Behavioral and Social Sciences, Research Report 1971, 2014.

Orvis, Bruce R., *Results and Implications of Selected Arroyo Center Research in Support of Army Recruiting*, unpublished RAND Corporation research, 2013.

Orvis, Bruce R., Michael Childress, and J. Michael Polich, *Effect of Personnel Quality on the Performance of Patriot Air Defense System Operators*, Santa Monica, Calif.: RAND Corporation, R-3901-A, 1992. As of November 3, 2017:
https://www.rand.org/pubs/reports/R3901.html

Orvis, Bruce R., Laurie L. McDonald, and Heather Krull, *Holistic Process for Increasing Deployability*, unpublished RAND Corporation research, 2012.

Orvis, Bruce R., Laurie L. McDonald, and Chung Pham, *Interim Results for Tier Two Attrition Screen Program*, unpublished RAND Corporation research, 2011.

Orvis, Bruce R., Sean Robson, Philip Hall-Partyka, and Tiffany Tsai, *Improvement of Special Forces Recruitment, Assessment and Selection, and Retention*, unpublished RAND Corporation research, 2015.

Otto, William C., David W. Niebuhr, Timothy E. Powers, Margot R. Krauss, Francis L. McVeigh, and Aaron K. Tarbett, "Attrition of Military Enlistees with a Medical Waiver for Myopia, 1999–2001," *Military Medicine*, Vol. 171, No. 11, 2006, pp. 1137–1141.

Packnett, Elizabeth R., David W. Niebuhr, Sheryl A. Bedno, and David N. Cowan, "Body Mass Index, Medical Qualification Status, and Discharge During the First Year of US Army Service," *American Journal of Clinical Nutrition*, Vol. 93, No. 3, 2011, pp. 608–614.

Putka, D. J., and K. M. Bradley, *Relations Between Select21 Predictor Measures and First-Term Attrition*, Arlington, Va.: U.S. Army Research Institute for the Behavioral and Social Sciences, 2008.

Quester, Aline O., *Marine Corps Recruits: A Historical Look at Accessions and Bootcamp Performance*, Alexandria, Va.: CNA, D0023537.A1, September 2010.

Sahin, Fatih, and Serhat Ayhan, *The Next Best Alternative to an Ideal Recruit: Attrition Characteristics of Recruits with Waivers and Low Educational Credentials in the U.S. Army*, Naval Postgraduate School, March 2009.

Salo, Mikael, and Guy L. Siebold, *Predictors of Attrition in the Finnish Conscript Service*, U.S. Army Research Institute for the Behavioral and Social Sciences, 2006.

Strickland, W. J., *A Longitudinal Examination of First Term Attrition and Reenlistment Among FY1999 Enlisted Accessions*, Arlington, Va.: U.S. Army Research Institute for the Behavioral and Social Sciences, 2005.

Turpin, Adam R., *Evaluating the Tailored Adaptive Personality Assessment System on Delayed Entry Program Attrition*, Master's thesis, Monterey, Calif.: Naval Postgraduate School, March 2014.

Vickers, R. R., Jr., L. K. Hervig, and R. F. Booth, *Personality and Success Among Military Enlisted Personnel: An Historical Prospective Study of U.S. Navy Corpsmen*, San Diego, Calif.: Naval Health Research Center, 1996.

Wenger, Jennie W., and Apriel K. Hodari, *Predictors of Attrition: Attitudes, Behaviors, and Educational Characteristics*, Alexandria, Va.: CNA, D0010146.A2, July 2004.

White, L. A., R. D. Nord, and F. A. Mael, *Setting Enlistment Standards on the ABLE to Reduce Attrition*, Arlington, Va.: U.S. Army Research Institute for the Behavioral and Social Sciences, 1990.

Winkler, John D., Judith C. Fernandez, and J. Michael Polich, *Effect of Aptitude on the Performance of Army Communications Operators*, Santa Monica, Calif.: RAND Corporation, R-4143-A, 1992. As of November 3, 2017: https://www.rand.org/pubs/reports/R4143.html

Zook, Lola M., *Soldier Selection: Past, Present and Future*, Arlington, Va.: U.S. Army Research Institute for the Behavioral and Social Sciences, 1996.